YOU ESSAY

SUPPLY-SIDE LIES
AND
THE MIDDLE CLASS DEMISE

[Writings from the mountains of Glacier National Park]

By Jerry Straka

Strategic Book Publishing and Rights Co.

Strategic Book Publishing and Rights Co.
12620 FM 1960, Suite A4-507
Houston TX 77065
www.spbra.com

ISBN: 978-1-61897-829-5

DEDICATION

"These are the times that try men's souls",
– from <u>Common Sense by Thomas Paine</u>.

To my twenty-something nieces and nephews; Derek, Sarah, Sam, Andy, Nathan, Danielle, John, Allison, Colby and Madeline. This book is for you. Though I have no children of my own, I think of each of you as mine.

Let me first acknowledge the failings of my generation. I thought we were better stewards, but many of my generation were fooled, and some were blinded by false promises. It was not our intent to burden you with our debt, or to leave you a jobless economy. Upon reading this, I hope you understand that some of us recognized the shortcomings of the policy decisions that caused this current mess, and we fervently fought for your future. You deserve an explanation. Your generation needs to know how we became the "99%".

ACKNOWLEDGEMENTS

Many of my friends and family encouraged me to write this book. My father and recently deceased mother showered me with years of unconditional love and support. I have truly been blessed. My five brothers, their wives, and my beautiful nieces and nephews, stood by me through thick and thin. Thank you all for your understanding.

Cheers: to my high school friend and fellow writer, Melanie, whose assistance is immensely useful, and whose friendship is a gift I cherish; and to my hiking and climbing friend, Dennis, who "has my back" when our adventures put us in harm's way. We'll share one soon.

Thank you to my local newspaper editors for publishing my essays over the years. Thanks Strategic Book Publishing for your patience and guidance with this "newbie" author. The professional approach and commitment to my project is immensely valued.

Lastly, my heartfelt appreciation to Glacier National Park and its employees, over the years you have welcomed me and given me refuge from the confusion. You facilitated my search for the meaning of life.

TABLE OF CONTENTS

INTRODUCTION

Abraham Lincoln wrote, *"Corporations have been enthroned and an era of corruption in high places will follow, and the money-power of the country will endeavor to prolong its reign by working upon the prejudices of the people until all wealth is aggregated in few hands and the republic is destroyed."*

and that republic is presently being destroyed.

***

[Letter to the editor: Great Falls Tribune]

What a nation of liars we've become. Thanks to thirty-five years of corporatism influence in our capitals, we lost all reason and became a country of polarized opinions waging war on each other with misinformation, disinformation, and outright lies.

Can anyone say that the loss of the Fairness Doctrine has given overworked citizens access to more truth? It is just the opposite, confusion reigns. Policy promotion depends upon the wordsmith's twisting of common language, eliciting the worst of human emotions. Fear and hate permeate the airwaves and common discourse. Thank you Fox News and Rush Limbaugh. We hunger for truth, but find few places that offer it. It's not by accident that we find ourselves here.

Corporate America got annoyed at the protests of the 1960's. Based upon the 'memorandum' by former Supreme Court justice Lewis Powell, a series of drastic changes were instituted. The memo influenced the creation of the Heritage Foundation, Citizens for a Sound Economy, Accuracy in Academe, the Manhattan Institute, the Cato Institute, ALEC, and other powerful organizations. They've promoted loyalty to party ideology rather than the Constitution. That's damned sad.

Since, we've witnessed the think tank attacks on all our cherished institutions such as the free press, capitalism, collective bargaining, education, family, and the right of dissent.

Jerry Straka
Whitefish, MT

Note: Lewis Franklin Powell, Jr was an Associate Justice of the Supreme Court of the United States. Based in part on his experiences as a corporate lawyer and as a representative for the tobacco industry with the Virginia legislature, he wrote the Powell Memorandum to a friend at the US Chamber of Commerce. The memo called for corporate America to become more aggressive in molding politics and law in the US and may have sparked the formation of one or more influential right-wing think tanks. (Source: Wikipedia)

PURPOSE

My sole purpose for publishing this book is to change the national conversation that has gotten so far out of whack. A false narrative riddled with factual incorrectness has been scripted and adhered to for decades now. It is the supply-side lie, and it's still being falsely promoted today.

Over the past thirty years, ideological propaganda has supplanted honest journalism. The demise of journalistic integrity is utterly staggering. Major news outlets no longer seek truth. They seek revenue, and truth be damned. Conflict sells, so reality is purposely blurred. Honest journalism has become the first casualty of deregulation. As a former journalist, I witnessed this decline firsthand.

What started during the Reagan years as misinformation and disinformation from the likes of Lee Atwater, Michael Deaver and Roger Ailes (now @ FOX News) has morphed into a divergent reality based on denial of fact, the incorrect rewriting of history, and the advocacy of disproven ideology, rather than truth seeking. Confusion reigns, on purpose, by design.

To recalibrate, let's start with these economic facts which are true and largely unreported.

1) Tax cuts cause deficits. Revenues as % of GDP are reduced, especially if GDP does not increase. Despite hundreds of false conservative claims, the Bush tax cuts did not pay for themselves (Source: Congressional Budget Office – further references listed as CBO). They caused massive deficits. No Republican ever proposed paying for them.

2) We have a revenue problem. Present revenues as a percent of GDP (<15%) are far below historic averages (<19%) (CBO). This is the seldom-reported serious problem. Revenues are at 60 year historic lows, during wartime. No Republican will admit this.

3) Our problem is not lack of capital for investment, rather lack of demand from falling wages and salaries. We have a demand problem, not a supply problem.

There are two distinctly separate conversations about the above facts. One side accepts the proof of the raw data (CBO, IRS, Dept. of

Labor statistics) and non-partisan findings. The other side still believes the Reagan and Bush tax cuts paid for themselves; revenues are not a problem; and that tax burdens are higher than thirty years ago. These assumptions have been proven blatantly false, yet they are never denied properly by a compliant corporate media. This factual incorrectness is tolerated, not corrected. That is why it is so crucial to insist on a fact-based conversation, to expose factual incorrectness, so problems can be properly defined and solved. Media bias and misuse must be exposed continually.

NEW TERMS

Two new terms may need further explanation. The first of these is scarerism. Scarerism is using propaganda to scare people into emotional reactions. Make them feel falsely threatened and tell them who is threatening. The second is hatriotism. Hatriotism is using propaganda to dishonestly pit average American against average American. Sadly, these are the weapons so commonly used in today's media environment, and they're working.

Supply-side Theory (def.)

An economic theory that holds that the reducing of tax rates, especially for businesses and wealthy individuals, stimulates savings and investment for the benefit of everyone. [Also called trickle-down economics or voodoo economics.]

Laffer Curve (def.)

Invented by Arthur Laffer, this curve shows the relationship between tax rates and tax revenue collected by governments. The curve suggests that, as taxes increase from low levels, tax revenue collected by the government also increases. It also shows that tax rates increasing after a certain point (T*) would cause people not to work as hard or not at all, thereby reducing tax revenue.

Note: The tax increases of the 1993 Deficit Reduction Act increased production; increased revenues and wages; and increased profits (CBO). This rendered moot and completely discredited the claim that tax increases have the aforementioned effect (i.e. revenue reduction). They had the opposite effect of outcomes predicted by Republican detractors who suggested the economy would suffer.

Fairness Doctrine: a policy of the United States Federal Communications Commission (FCC), introduced in 1949, that required the holders of broadcast licenses to present controversial issues of public importance and to do so in a manner that was, in the Commission's view, honest, equitable and balanced.

The following writings address concerns about two significant changes that have taken place since 1980. One is the introduction of supply-side economics, and the other is media consolidation. One will find that my views strongly condemn the status quo in our media and corporate cultures, both areas of my undergraduate and graduate studies in business and journalism. The additional historical renderings are for contextual purposes.

This is a system not easily changed from within. It is too corrupt. Change needs to come from outside the "DC box".

HOW IT BEGAN – AND THE BACKLASH WE STILL FEEL TODAY

Climbing inside the collective mind of the ultra-wealthy, privileged industrialists of the 1970's requires a journey into a world where hate, vindictiveness, and oppressive recourse rule. These elitists felt under attack (see Powell Memo) and they bristled with hatred. No one was going to tell them what to do, no draft protesters, no media investigators, no civil rights activists, no unions, no EPA, no one. Their reaction is a lesson in child psychology. They hold lifelong grudges and engage in relentless retaliation.

The backlash came in the guise of the Powell memorandum. It nurtured protester hatred, union hatred, media hatred, environmentalist hatred, hippie hatred, welfare hatred (thinly veiled racism), and it utterly consumed the wealthy class during the Vietnam fiasco. Damn it, they'd had enough, so they organized and began a propaganda campaign that still exists today, against all their perceived enemies. The weapon they chose was money. They sought to control the government through lobbying/campaign financing and the media through consolidation and deregulation (90% of all media owned by five corporations). They invested to shut out the unions by plant closings/relocations as part of globalization. Through intense investment in unregulated economies abroad, they have polluted vast areas to an extent unseen since the onset of the EPA. The plan was to do anything they damn well pleased, as long it resulted in profit. Screw Americans. And Ronald Reagan was to become their standard bearer.

The war against the government, the war against the media, the war against labor, the war against public education, and the war against the Constitution was waged against the unsuspecting masses. War rooms operated deep in the bowels of newly established and heavily funded think tanks. The offensive required the establishment of WMD, weapons of mass deceit.

New, unproven theories were to be advanced (disinformation), and old arguments were to be defended with deceit (misinformation). Reality was viewed as a concept that could be manipulated through careful public relations efforts incorporating fear, hate, distrust, and lies. Divide and conquer. Only the outcome mattered. The means and the lack of moral or ethical purpose mattered not. Intentionally or not decency became the victim of these actions.

"There's class warfare, all right, but it's my class, the rich class, that's making war, and we're winning." (Nov. 2006) Warren Buffet (America's richest man)

***

Obviously, the main premise of this book is the evolution of the class warfare that had long been present, but was consolidated in the memorandum by Lewis Powell. Upon perusal of the memorandum, people will come to understand that in order to implement Powell's strategies it would become necessary to deceive the masses. How does one get people to vote against their own economic interests? One promotes supply-side economic theory and the now discredited Laffer curve.

Once one chooses to leave the path of honesty and decency, subsequent falsehoods become easier to promote and defend. Just as fast as our deficit has ballooned from the onset of the supply-side lie, so have the reasons/excuses for its apparent shortcomings.

A vicious pattern of deceit, an alternative reality, a false narrative, has replaced reason and truth. Paid propagandists promote the think-tank derived daily talking points with a fervor and hatred unseen in previous generations. Dissent is treated as treason and honest policy disagreements are labeled unpatriotic. Welcome HATE radio. Goodbye intellectual integrity.

Let's step back to the initial implementation of this thinking on a national level. When the 1980 election came around we were driving 55 mph and setting our thermostats at 68 degrees because of an energy crisis. Vehicles sported "Buy American" stickers in response to Japanese automakers grabbing increasingly large shares of the market. Interest rates and unemployment were both near double digits. The credit card industry was emergent. There was much uncertainty.

Then along comes Reagan armed with the supply-side lie, Reaganomics. There was steady economic improvement, as the computer industry boomed. There were also junk bonds, the S&L crisis, bailouts, LBO's with pension raids, and whopping deficits. With these problems came a slow decline from fact to fiction, or ideology protection.

By the time Reagan left office, those "Buy American" bumper stickers were gone; deregulated Wall Street ruled; the credit card industry flourished; we were financing growth through deficits; drilling for energy independence was promoted as a viable policy as speed limits were increased; and in an astonishing display of arrogance, the solar panels were removed from the White House at the personal request of President Reagan.

The revolution was on. Lewis Powell's manifesto professing more corporate control was in full swing. In one of Reagan's last acts, ridding us of the Fairness Doctrine, the door opened for control of media messages by recently deregulated, consolidated corporate owners. I give you Fox News, Rush Limbaugh, Hannity, Coulter, O'Reilly, Savage, Beck, et al and the venomous partisan political discourse it spawned.

By 2002, I realized Lincoln's warning of corporate rule had reached fruition. The Supreme Court appointed a corporate President and the corporate agenda was pursued vigorously. With the corporate coup complete, the propaganda machine was cranked up to the max. Lies, so many lies. The Orwellian "Ministry of Truth" narrative became deafening.

VIEWS AND PERSPECTIVES

I had to get away and sort it out. So I began climbing and hiking more, and reading and researching economics more. Answers weren't coming from our leaders or supposed 'unbiased' media. So I chose reflection by exploring Glacier Park, witnessing glaciers disappear.

Communing with nature cleanses the mind. On mountaintops and in mountain streams, answers await discovery. They have for millennia. There is no better way of achieving clarity of thought than disappearing into the wilderness or climbing atop a mountain. The exercise has many levels. It is not just the ultimate destination, but rather the hardships encountered and effort extended that lead to the satisfaction and inner calm at journey's end. The respites offer focus and reflection. The accomplishments reward purpose. It's as real as real gets.

HIDDEN LAKE

Of all the beauty in Glacier Park, of all the places to see and explore, the one place that keeps calling me back is Hidden Lake. This mile and a half long lake, tucked just over the continental divide from the Logan Pass parking lot, is surrounded by monumental peaks. It is three miles to the shore, half uphill to the overlook and half downhill to the lake. One traverses the continental divide; crossing streams that empty north into the Hudson Bay and streams that empty west into the Pacific Ocean. The uphill, from the Logan Pass visitor center, is packed with tourists all season. Few wander past the overlook and venture downhill to the lakeshore, knowing the climb out is arduous. Even fewer cross the knee deep, fifty foot wide, chilling outlet to follow the shoreline to the lakes other end. On many occasions, I've seen no other person as I fished for hours the rocky shorelines beyond the outlet.

My first hike into the Hidden Lake was almost thirty years ago. Since, I've visited its shores at least another seventy-five times. It is my "Fortress of Solitude". On perhaps half of those visits, I've hiked alone, on purpose. It was not my fellow man I wished to be with on those days. It was the other creatures whose company I sought, and they always seem to welcome me.

One cannot hike up the boardwalk and trail to the Hidden Lake overlook without encountering mountain goats. Never have I hiked into Hidden Lake without seeing mountain goats. When the nannies are accompanied by their month's old kids, it's as beautiful as beautiful gets. It is total innocence surrounded by absolute magnificence. Juxtaposed against melting snowfields spawning crystal clear streams, amongst a bloomy array most florists would envy, with a backdrop of seemingly endless jagged peaks, the mountain goat flourishes and thrives. What a welcoming committee as one enters nirvana.

Other creatures compete for attention. Bighorn sheep, less docile than goats, tend to form genders groups and the rams visit the high mountain meadows for sustenance and sunshine. During their frequent cantankerous moments, they position for advantage before colliding together. When two Bighorn rams meet from a distance of only a few yards, the echo of their horns clashing is near thunderous. A spectacular event.

Marmots, Columbian ground squirrels, and pika inhabit the rocky boulder and scree fields, chirping out warnings as others come near. Perfectly camouflaged Ptarmigan and their chicks disappear into the landscape just feet away from where they were last. Overhead, the golden eagles dwarf the smaller bald eagles or osprey, and on those very special days, special to me at least, one can have a grizzly encounter. But the most exceptional encounter of all, an encounter that I've been blessed to experience on numerous occasions, is that with a wolverine and its kits.

Hidden Lake was stocked with Yellowstone Cutthroat trout nearly a century ago by Great Northern Railroad. Many of the lakes in Glacier Park had non-native species introduced in the early days (early 1900's) of the Park. The trout in Hidden Lake spawn in the outlet when the ice leaves the lake (mid-late July). Once that spawn has ended, they are voracious feeders and fighters. Growing over 20 inches in length and over 3 pounds in weight, these fish cruise the shorelines offering themselves to the wily angler who can determine which bait they hunger for that day.

In the summer of 2002, as I stood alone upon the shoreline coaxing a reluctant trout, there was a flurry and rustle behind me in the brush. I turned to see the commotion and there staring right back were two wolverine kits. If one has never seen a wolverine, one would be pleasantly unafraid of this supposed predator. They exude a certain raccoon curiosity and playfulness. I've never felt threatened in the numerous encounters with my wolverine friends at Hidden Lake, and we've had many an encounter over the years since.

On this occasion, while I fished a brushy shoreline across the outlet, the kits were only checking me out. When I put my fishing pole down to grab my camera, they quickly hid in the underbrush, out of view. I'd wait, and then return to fishing. They would come again. I'd put the pole down; they'd disappear. I'd start fishing; they'd reappear. We played this game for nearly an hour. I could almost hear their laughter as I was fooled over and over again.

I eventually tracked them to their den (on another day) and discovered over the years that this den site, away from the shore and tucked into a rock pile beneath Bearhat Mountain, was used most every year. Not every year, but more than not. I miss them when then gone, but so enjoy them when they are present. There are times when only their interaction can fulfill my needs, because it means that nothing else matters. I seek that mindset to clear my thoughts.

The pinnacles that surround Hidden Lake are spectacular. Mount Clements, Bearhat Mountain, Mount Cannon, Dragon's Tail, and Mount Reynolds are all former destinations of mine. I've climbed Mount Reynolds over a dozen times to take in one of the most beautiful summit views on earth. The peak rises about a half mile in elevation above the meadows of Logan Pass and Going-to-the-Sun Road and offer Lake and Logan Pass views. St. Mary Lake can be seen to the east and Lake McDonald to the west. Awesome, but the lake view that captures my eye the most is that of looking over half a mile straight down into Hidden Lake from any of these summits. Words cannot describe, and pictures can only hint at the setting below. It has to be experienced.

Whether the days venture is to climb or to fish, the Hidden Lake landscape is full of places to explore. The peninsula-ridden shoreline is blanketed to the water's edge with glacier lilies, monkey flowers, asters, buttercups, forget-me-nots, and dozens of other floral creations. The grown-over user path to the far backside of the lake is part of a fifteen mile cross-country conduit, to Sperry Chalet, that skirts Sperry Glacier and passes far above the Avalanche Lake basin through a meadow of such beauty it is known as Floral Park. The user trail crosses dozens of streams and past hundreds of waterfalls. There are so many waterfalls from the melting snowfields, that I believe it near impossible to find them all. They are everywhere, in every cranny, in every nook, and sometimes suddenly appearing from the dry ground beneath your feet. And does that water refresh! WOW! It is as pure as it gets, filtered through the mountain from the snowfield just above. All gathered in an orchestrated symphony of fluid motion and misty release. It is the water that separates Glacier Park from other destinations. The water is so pure in some places that remote Glacier Park lakes are used as keystone lakes for determining water purity.

Following the streams uphill to the snowfields, and reaching the ridge tops beyond only to witness another most wondrous mountain valley that most will never see, is a journey of discovery, both outward and inward. Just as you come to realize that nature's every detail seems in place, you come to realize that you are part of it. In those moments, it opens up a consciousness that isn't always accessible amongst the clutter of humanity.

Yes, a day at Hidden Lake is always good therapy. I call it my own personal "Jerapy". It is my place for deep reflection.

These moments of reflection resulted in the following dated essays published by my regional newspapers (Great Falls Tribune, Missoulian, The Daily InterLake) over the last ten years. They are perspectives written for the common person from uncommon places. They are observations of current events from an "outside view".

Enjoy the views and perspectives.

Hidden Lake and Mount Reynolds "spire" as seen from Bearhat
Mt. summit – photo by author

WELCOME TO THE PLUTOCRACY

A foretelling letter…..

(November 2002)

It's official. We now live in a plutocracy. The Republicans have political control. Their campaign of misinformation, disinformation, and opposition demonizing has succeeded. What will the next years bring?

First, the Constitution will become a Republican doormat. Conservative judges have already gutted your fourth amendment rights and will continue to do so. What good is your right to bear arms if you lose your rights against search and seizure? Privacy rights will be compromised for security reasons. Despite the fact that the Constitution specifically calls for regulation of commerce, Republicans will deregulate everything conceivable. They have to pay back big contributors. Hence, corporate crime will increase, but we won't know because no one will be policing it. What good are laws with no enforcement? Few corporate criminals will do time, which is shameful. Separation of church and state? Gone. Faith-based initiatives will prevail to pay back the Christian right for their support. Congress's constitutionally granted duty to declare war has already been tested and ignored by this Republican administration.

Further, anyone who questions the Republican rush to deregulate environmental laws will be labeled a radical eco-terrorist and anyone who questions Republican go-it-alone foreign policy will be labeled unpatriotic.

Lastly, the future will be mortgaged by increased government debt and continued raiding of Social Security funds as a result of even more corporate and top 1% tax breaks. This puts more burdens on the wage earners, those with income of $100,000 or less. Ah, life in a plutocracy. Can it get any better?

Jerry Straka

***

Nine years later…..

(November 2011)

The Boston Tea Party was a protest against the British government and the monopolistic East India Company that controlled all the tea imported into the colonies. It was a protest against corporate interests condoned and imposed by a dynastic government.

Fast forward 245 years and we have Occupy Wall Street, a real tea party, not a tea party promoted by corporate media (Fox News) and funded by a handful of billionaires and their corporate money (Americans for Prosperity). Occupy Wall Street is not contrived over false issues. TEA - Taxed Enough Already. Really? Taxes had just been reduced for 98 percent of Americans. Taxes are at their lowest level in over sixty years (CBO). Death panels? Voted the biggest lie of 2009 by numerous non-partisan media groups. Socialism? More like corporate scarerism. No, Occupy Wall Street is real, spontaneous, and multifaceted, yet single-purposed. It is a response to those same corporate interests condoned and imposed by the government that were the basis of the original Boston Tea Party. This movement is very real and long overdue.

The dynamics of capital vs. labor and of laws of supply and demand have been around for centuries. Multinational corporations and their dynastic ownership, the financial elite, understand these and have devised decade's-long plans for their sole benefit. First, through political influence (bribes), they increased the tax on US labor by 50 percent and cut in half the US tax on capital. Class warfare began with Reaganomics. Second, with these windfall profits, they consolidated and merged to concentrate wealth and reduce market participants under the guise of deregulation. Teddy Roosevelt's anti-trust provisions were gutted in the 1980s and 1990s. Many markets are now dominated by anti-capitalistic, oligopoly rule, with fewer and fewer competitors, just what Roosevelt fought against.

The elites then sought the untapped labor in burgeoning Third World markets. Trade deals were developed and promoted that benefitted their pursuit of this labor, albeit to the detriment of the remaining patriotic others who remained here. Why would we negotiate trade deals where exports are taxed at rates up to ten times higher than their counterpart imports? The reason is that politically powerful multinationals had the resources to move and export. They had no desire to compete against remaining American competitors, so they hamstrung them with trade barriers. Paid politicians from both parties promoted and passed these trade laws. This forced normally patriotic US companies to relocate in order to compete. Forty thousand factories have closed and relocated overseas since 2001 (source: www.businessinsider.com/deindustrialization). Recent trade policy has nothing to do with opening markets for American made goods shipped abroad. Rather, it is all about opening markets for American companies to relocate abroad. These policy implementations have gutted our manufacturing base and strengthened our competitors. As Ross Perot described it in 1992, it is "a giant sucking sound" of American jobs being exported. This is shameful, un-American, despicable behavior that was devised decades ago by the wealthiest of Americans.

The biggest obstacle for these dynastic families has always been getting regular Americans to vote against their own economic self-interests. How does one get Americans to willingly give up their jobs and economic security? How does one get the 99% to support policies that benefit only the top 1%? How does one do it? Simply put, by lying.

The plutocracy funds think tanks like the American Enterprise Institute, Heritage Foundation, Cato Institute, American Legislative Exchange Council-ALEC, etc., whose research goals result in predetermined, false outcomes that heavily favor corporate interests. Then they pay (bribe) politicians through campaign donations and lobbying (more bribes) to sell these predetermined, false outcomes to the masses. They promote failed, disproven policies like supply-side economics and financial deregulation while blaming the nation's woes on the poorest Americans. Through media consolidation and its deregulation, they limit the impact of any opposition, any independent journalistic voices, by buying them out and replacing them with personalities who spew ideology, not fact. These personalities are paid well and are fully scripted to pit average American against average American. They are paid to manufacture false conflict among the masses, while the top 1% robs us blind. And it's working.

Zealots don tea bags, tote guns, and scream of income redistribution while their incomes have stagnated for the last thirty years; while their personal wealth and homes are stolen through corporate mortgage fraud; while their prepaid health and retirement benefits are being taken away to fund unpaid, unnecessary wars; and while their jobs and children's future are shipped abroad. All this while the top 1% tripled their income and hoarded trillions in cash overseas.

I really think the Tea Party acronym should stand for Take Everything Away, not Taxed Enough Already. Somehow they have become willing soldiers for the Godless money-changers Jesus despised. They blame and malign the poor for the excesses of the wealthy. That is not Christian, not by my Bible.

That is why there is an Occupy Wall Street. The occupiers are onto the incessant lies and false promises. They are tired of the constant deceit and fear-mongering. They are saying, ENOUGH! They don't believe that the bottom 50% have caused this problem. The bottom 50% has neither the financial means nor the organizational capacity to commit the fraud for which the Tea Party and their corporate masters blame them.

Occupy Wall Street doesn't believe that corporations are persons and that money is speech. C'mon Tea Party, this is right up your alley. Foreign born, un-naturalized citizens with no birth certificates that live in mail boxes on islands. They are not even mentioned in the Constitution, even though they were abundant in 1776 and were primarily responsible for the protest called the Boston Tea Party. They were excluded from the Constitution on purpose. On Purpose! Please, Tea Party. Get on the right side of this one.

Occupy Wall Street sees through the corporate dominance of the government and our media. Theirs is the real manifestation of the Tea Party's misplaced anger put to proper use against the real villains of our financial malady: the top 1% and their corporate shields and shills, those who control 40% of our wealth and tens of trillions, not the bottom 50%, who control only 2.5% of wealth with cumulative holdings of only $1.5 trillion (IRS).

Call them mobs (Representative Eric Cantor), call them un-American (Herman Cain), call it class warfare (Mitt Romney and others), call it whatever one wants. These people are used to being called names. Don't expect them to leave until Wall Street thieves go to jail for mortgage fraud and repay their victims; until corporate money is removed from politics and corporate citizenship is rescinded; until fair trade deals are adopted that benefit capital and labor and the environment; or until investment is made in American roads, bridges, energy/power grid, schools, and its own people rather than in those countries we just destroyed.

I have ten beautiful, intelligent nieces and nephews of employment age and another three recently adopted young ones, bless my brother and his wife. Most have college degrees, some advanced degrees, some still in college choosing majors. I worry about their future every day, but I cannot, and will not, tell them that a jobless future was the result of income redistribution to the poor when it was exactly the opposite. I cannot, and will not, tell them that over-regulation caused the housing crisis that gutted their parent's wealth and their inheritance when even Alan Greenspan says it was quite the opposite. I cannot, and will not, tell them that overpaying teachers, nurses, firemen, and union members caused our financial crisis when these wages stagnated over the last thirty years. I cannot, and will not, blame my middle-class America friends and neighbors for this, except that they trusted corporate America. They should not have then, and they should not now.

That's what Occupy Wall Street and its growing participation is all about, the truth. It's about putting the blame where it belongs by putting an end to state-sanctioned, politically corrupt, corporate rule by the elite, few, dynastic families. Just like the Boston Tea Party.

Jerry Straka

ON THE ECONOMY

(December 2002)

Sometimes lessons are never learned. The last time conservatives controlled the White House and parts of Congress we (wage earners of $100,000/yr. and less) found our pocketbooks emptied; to pay for deregulation in the Savings & Loan (half a trillion dollars); to pay for over two trillion dollars in accumulated debt; to pay for massive tax cuts for corporations and their owners.

Eleven times in those twelve Republican submitted budgets during the Reagan/Bush era Congress allocated less than submitted (CBO). There goes the Congress was the fault argument. Now we have another supply-sider (G.W. Bush) promising the same old/same old while emptying the Treasury faster than one can shake a stick.

Recently, conservatives have passed legislation allowing corporate shell off-shore mailbox locations to continue to avoid billions in taxes yearly despite the public outcry against such practices. They claim its only business trying to cut costs. Well, when business buys legislation through campaign donations, unfairly benefitting a few, many of us see it as corruption.

Has anyone gone to jail for the largest organized theft in U. S. history, the costly multitrillion dollar scams on Wall Street? Few served time for the Savings & Loan failures. I expect few will do time for these latest crimes. Laws will be changed making unethical acts legal, and other laws will not be enforced. That 401K hit hurts a little worse when the thieves go free. Plus, who wants to invest in a perceived rigged system?

Now we hear that further tax cuts, mostly corporate tax rebates, often paid to corporations that never paid taxes to begin with, are being considered to spark economic activity. Open up the pocketbooks again wage-earners.

I guess the lessons of the 80's didn't register to most voters.

***

(June 2003)

In recent weeks, I've heard many conservatives claim that non-passage of an economic stimulus package is unpatriotic. The blame throwers are at it again.

Do we need to prime the corporate pump more? Until demand increases from the consumer level, jobs and inventories will get no new investment. Basic business principles include minimizing factors of production (i.e. labor, taxes). Business always works to reduce these costs. Hence no jobs created yet from last year's record tax break. Demand has not increased to justify the investment. Since the record tax break; Motorola has axed 40,000 jobs; Ford has axed 25,000 jobs; the airlines purged another 100,000; Enron, let's not go there; and that's the tip of the iceberg. We're told by conservatives that without massive corporate tax cuts like those given last spring, jobs will not be created. Hmm. Fact is we live in a demand economy that requires new solutions. Tired supply-side answers will do nothing but empty the coffers and increase deficits as they did in the '80's.

Those who try to eliminate the law requiring corporations to pay at least a minimal tax, those espousing corporate tax rebates, should be wary of wrapping themselves in the flag as they spew patriotic rhetoric. This is just business minimizing costs again. It has nothing to do with job creation. It has to do with corporate contributions to political campaigns that have subverted our political process. This existing corporate/campaign finance paradigm must be shifted away from such heavy influence.

***

(August 2003)

I guess I'm a liberal. I don't believe that targeted tax breaks to the wealthy create jobs. As a former MBA student, my studies revealed that these tax breaks were never proven to create jobs. Further proof is the net loss of three million jobs in the last two years. A social security tax holiday for small business puts money in the hand of the real job creators.

I don't believe that a $500 million fine and no admission of guilt for World.com, who bilked their investors of $11 billion, are getting tough on corporate criminals. Nor is a $50 million fine with no guilt admission fair for Merrill Lynch's part in knowingly misstating Enron's financials. Put these people in jail, damn it.

I don't believe spending $50 billion a year to rebuild Iraq is more important than the $40 billion spent on Homeland Security. Protect us, conservatives. We're more important than Cheney's oil. I have yet to be convinced that the promised savings of deregulation will be realized. Every deregulated industry (i.e. energy, banking, and accounting) has raised prices and cut services.

I don't believe in corporate welfare. Risk is part of business. Reducing risk by reaching into taxpayer's pockets for bailouts is class warfare; waged and started by this administration.

Lastly, I strongly disagree with continuing conservative policy allowing off-shore corporate mailbox location to avoid taxes. These lost revenues instead are taken from the wage earners pocket. More class warfare. I guess I'm a liberal.

***

(October 2003)

Universal basic business principles, as taught in all undergraduate and graduate level business classes, stress minimizing factors of production (i.e. raw materials, taxes, inventories, labor).

Let's say one owns a widget factory that supplies many vehicle makers and orders and revenues are down. Inventories are overstocked. What does one do? Answer. One cuts hours or lays off part of the workforce and reduces inventories until demand increases, basic business.

Now Pres. Bush says he's giving massive tax breaks to create jobs. Does one hire back those laid off? Absolutely not. Until demand increases, one operates at less than 100%. This minimizes capital in inventories and labor and maximizes profits.

Supply side theory as practiced by this President is a colossal lie. How many times have conservatives echoed that problems aren't solved by throwing money at them, unless, it seems, the money goes to wealthy conservative backers. Here's another reason to end private campaign financing.

Limbaugh, Hannity, O'Reilly (pick a blow horn) preach this same nonsense because they're paid to, by the same aforementioned backers. Were opposing voices truly allowed on these propaganda programs, were policy debate ever given a fair chance, people would overwhelmingly reject Bush's deficit growing, wealthy coddling, future mortgaging tax cut plan.

Bush is spending one billion dollars a day to make war with whom he pleases; paying coalition members tens of billions of dollars to back us; and spending an additional $40 billion on Homeland security. Added to the record tax cuts that resulted in two million lost jobs in 2001 (Dept. of Labor), Bush proposes $750+ billion in new tax cuts for the wealthiest Americans, the very same people who cost the economy trillions in corporate crime. This is insane to reward thieves during wartime.

***

(April 2004)

Middle class Americans unite. Class warfare has been declared and is being waged in the halls of Congress by the privileged aristocracy. The agenda they seek is fourfold: rid society of any government oversight of business or labor, creating a new plantation/slave relationship; replace a progressive tax system, espoused by Ben Franklin and Abraham Lincoln, with a regressive tax system that burdens the lower classes; legislatively create a system where corporate capital has more rights than human labor; and remove any recourse available to dissenters (i.e. information access, assembly and protest rights, free speech and most every other bill of rights amendment).

This group doesn't allow internal dissent or external debate. Deceit, intimidation, fear and hate are their main weapons. They heavily fund think tanks for the sole purpose of creating disinformation/misinformation for dissemination on talk radio/cable. If one questions their methodology, assumptions or findings, one is shouted down and called names. They believe capitalism should have no rules; the strong get stronger and the weak get crushed. If one cannot win fairly, bribe the officials, sabotage the opponents, or cheat. Tilting the field to their unfair advantage is part of the game, kind of "it's not wrong if you don't caught" or better yet "it's not wrong if you deny it" mindset. To top it off these people lay claim to God. It's time to rid ourselves of this irresponsible aristocracy. It's time to fight back.

***

(July 2004)

Conservative fiscal policy has been a topic I've written about frequently, and as we approach another election it's time to examine it again. A recently released Republican-controlled Congressional Budget Office (CBO) report confirmed what I and many others have predicted in this paper. Taxes on those making less than $80,000/yr. and more than $40,000/yr. have increased, and taxes on those making less than $40,000/yr. have remained close to the same despite enormous increases in fuel, insurance, tuition, and food prices. A tax burden shift of this size hasn't happened since Reagan, who with the help of Alan Greenspan's commission raised Social Security and Medicare contributions by over 35% in the 1980's.

As Wall Street boasts record profits not witnessed since the 1920's, job creation lags, wages remain stagnant, company pension participation wanes, and health coverage declines. In the meantime, corporate tax contributions declined to a historic low of 7.4% of revenues (IRS). That's about a quarter of what they were during the 1950's boom when demand-side economics prevailed. A record $1 trillion surplus has been replaced in three short years by a $1 trillion deficit with no end of red ink in sight. Our children thank you for the debt. And this is responsible governing?

In my many years of continuing business education, no credible person has been able to defend this lunacy called supply-side. Yet conservatives continue to embrace this failed policy despite overwhelming evidence that it just doesn't work. It's simply a ruse to shift the tax burden, nothing else.

If any local radio station is willing, I'll gladly discuss this with any Republican brave enough to defend conservative supply-side policy. Really. Some of us would like to get an explanation of what further proposed tax cuts to the wealthy and to corporations will do for average Americans. Some of us would like the truth.

***

(January 2006)

Permanent tax cuts. As we face record deficits with no end in sight, a war in Iraq projected to cost well over 1 trillion dollars (that's trillion), government spending increasing faster than any time in history, and substantial job cuts in manufacturing and technology (i.e. Ford, GM, Microsoft, Boeing), the President is requesting further tax cuts for the wealthy.

Can the supply-side argument. That puppy won't hunt. U.S companies are awash with capital but are not investing it in America or Americans. Companies are investing in India, Mexico, South Korea, and unbelievably in Communist China at record levels. The transfer of technology to Communist China threatens future competitiveness and security, but U.S. companies and U.S Congressmen can't book flights fast enough to exploit cheap, sweat-shop labor and lax environmental standards.

Yes, Communist Cuba and Socialist Venezuela are demonized and even threatened by religious and political leaders. Conversely, nuclear power Communist China is embraced with open arms and lavished with business concessions (i.e. Google and Yahoo have modified search engines to censor free speech and access).

People, American political and business leadership is ethically bankrupt to continue these practices for the simple pursuit of maximizing profits. This short-mindedness creates dire consequences. Beside burgeoning deficits, dangerous technology transfers, and growing trade imbalances, the middle-class is quickly disappearing due to stagnant wage growth and exploitation of cheap labor abroad and at home.

Meanwhile, the rich get richer. Non-wage income is taxed at lower rates (i.e. capital gains, dividends); loopholes get bigger; and pension funds are stolen to reward shareholders, rather than pay stakeholders. Well, President Bush, cut the taxes to starve the beast, burden our children with debt and enjoy the spoils. Americans will not forget.

***

(March 2006)

To all Republicans, conservatives, and listeners of talk radio. Newsflash, not all people who disagree with your economic and foreign policy vision are proponents of some hate radio contrived liberal group. There are extremely persuasive arguments by opponents of supply-side economics and preemptive war. Recent books by life-long, highly respected Republicans such as Bruce Bartlett, Imposter, and former Nixon staffer Kevin Phillips, American Dynasty: Aristocracy, Fortune, and the Politics of Deceit in the House of Bush, outline convincing arguments and poignantly describe the ever growing rift within the Republican Party.

Says Bruce Barlett; "Having worked in the (Republican) White House, at the Treasury Department, and in the House and Senate, I have a pretty good idea of how the policy development system should operate. It involves serious study and analysis of important issues, consultation with outside experts and Congress, and an open and transparent system for review and input from the public and affected parties. This White House will have none of that. Policies are developed on the fly and in secret with little or no analysis or forethought, and then rammed through a compliant Congress, often without anyone knowing the full details. This is a bad system that leads to mistakes, most obviously in the case of the inept implementation of the prescription drug program. Although I do not explicitly draw this connection in the book, I think many of our problems in Iraq are also due to a poor policy development process."

When asked, what went wrong with Bush's tax cuts? Barlett responded; "I think there was never any plan for what the tax cuts were supposed to achieve substantively. Many of the provisions enacted are the tax-equivalent of pork-barrel spending, which lost a lot of revenue while doing little or nothing to increase economic growth or improve the structure of the tax system."

Says Kevin Phillips; "Three generations of immersion in the culture of secrecy...deceit and disinformation have become Bush political hallmarks...... when you get the Bushes; you get really what amounts to a four-generation history of involvement with finance and the oil industry. That's what they've done. They haven't done much else. And their loyalties are enormous toward, first off, an economics of investors and inheritors, as opposed to workers and earners; and, secondly, a very close tie to the intelligence agencies of the military-industrial complex, of which the oil industry has become a major part. Obviously, there are the ties to the oil industry and the preoccupation with the Middle East and Texas, and the price of oil. There again, that's a bias which is both economic and geographic."

Also, from that interview with BuzzFlash, Phillips says, "Entitlement, elitism, privilege, secrecy, mediocrity, corruption, financial cronyism, bailouts of family failures by the taxpayers -- these are some of the true characteristics of the Bush Dynasty, according to Phillips."

Further proof of disagreements with the Bush policies comes from his Council of Economic Advisors. Former Bush CEA head, conservative economist Glenn Hubbard, stated in 2003 in response to continued tax cuts that the economy "is unlikely to grow so much that lost revenue is completely recovered by the higher level of economic activity". Another conservative economist and former head of the Bush administration's CEA, N. Gregory Mankiw, wrote there is "no credible evidence" that tax cuts pay for themselves. Mr. Mankiw also compared people who support this theory to "snake oil salesmen who are trying to sell a miracle cure".

Now, I'm sure that no one would consider these opponents to the Bush policies as liberal. So, please understand Republicans, conservatives and listeners of talk radio, not all criticism is the result of gay marriage backing, pro-abortion, tree-hugging, liberals who are anti-American. If one would take the time to read conservative doctrine, one would know.

***

(April 2006)

On previous occasions, I've written to address the issue of the tax policy of President Bush and the Republican Party. It is based on the yet unproven theory of supply side economics. While an MBA graduate student at the University of Montana and since, I've spent countless hours researching and analyzing the processes behind this theory. How can tax cuts increase government revenues? Granted, if it is assured that the money gained from tax breaks is directly invested into taxable revenue-producing activities in the U. S., this should theoretically grow the pie and create an increase in revenues, given that the size of the tax cut is not larger than the projected gains in revenue.

Here within lie two problems. (1) There is no assurance that these tax breaks will be invested in revenue producing activities and

(2) at some point revenue gains will not offset the huge loss created by those tax breaks. In other words, a tax rate of zero begets zero. One cannot cut taxes forever. So where is that breakeven point?

Republicans will have one believe that we have not reached that point, that more tax breaks means larger economic growth rates and that this "theory" is perpetual. They keep saying we'll grow our way beyond the breakeven point, even though the economic growth they project is unsustainable if even achievable in the first place. Trust us they say.

Here's what I trust. The President's own Council of Economic Advisers (CEA), headed by conservative economist Glenn Hubbard, stated in 2003 in response to continued tax cuts that the economy "is unlikely to grow so much that lost revenue is completely recovered by the higher level of economic activity". Hence, greater deficits. Another conservative economist and former head of the Bush administration's CEA, N. Gregory Mankiw, wrote (in a 1998 textbook) there is "no credible evidence" that tax cuts pay for themselves. That is why I previously stated that supply-side is an unproven theory. The data just doesn't support the claim. Furthermore, Mr. Mankiw compared people who support this theory to "snake oil salesmen who are trying to sell a miracle cure".

All I ask Republicans and their supporters to do are listen to your own economists. Bush's former Treasury secretary Paul O'Neill was fired for listening and speaking out about this advice. Seems the snake oil salesmen don't like dissent. Our elected officials, however, can be persuaded by a well-informed constituency that further cuts for the wealthy will only weaken the economy by increasing our deficit. Please Republicans tell our representatives to put the politics of tax cuts aside. Be wise fiscal managers. Don't burden our children with debt.

**

(August 2007)

"Where the hell is our outrage?........We've got a gang of clueless bozos steering our ship of state right over a cliff, we've got corporate gangsters stealing us blind....but instead of getting mad, everyone sits around and nods their heads when the politicians say, 'Stay the course.' Stay the course? You've got to be kidding. This is America, not the damned Titanic".

From <u>Where Have All the Leaders Gone?</u>, by Lee Iacocca.

I agree wholeheartedly. Especially the corporate gangsters part. Corporations have been granted personhood by radical right court decisions. The same judges ruled money is speech. With all these new persons and their speech, the rest of the electorate has essentially been disenfranchised. Using this power, Corporate America reduced their taxes from 28% of federal revenues in the late 1950's to less than 10% today (IRS). Citizen taxpayers make up that loss. Our manufacturing base has been given to China and India. Immigration policy is a joke. There is no immigration policy when the borders are open for corporate business's lust for cheap labor. Benefits are reduced yearly, and pensions are raided in takeovers at taxpayer expense. Fake science is financed to tear down our educational institutions; that's just criminal. There's war profiteering, markets are rigged by insiders, accounting scandals, etc.

Corporate America abandoned America for short term profit and has lied about it every inch of the way. It's time to regulate commerce again as the Constitution states and make these persons obey the laws like the rest of us.

***

(March 2008)

With the Dow dropping below 12,000, perhaps it's time to examine the Bush/Cheney fiscal record. The day they took office the Dow was at 10,578 and NASDAQ was 2757. After seven years of supply-side, NASDAQ (now 2212) has lost almost 20% and the Dow a slight 12% gain.

When Reagan took office the federal deficit was less than $800 billion, and increased to $5.7 trillion by Jan. 2001. Bush/Cheney inherited a yearly budget surplus that would have paid off all debt by 2010 by following the fiscal policy in place (CBO). Now, estimates are that the deficit will surpass $10 trillion before these fools leave office. Gas was about $1.50/gal and $30/barrel. It is now $3.20/gal and over $100/barrel. Real wages, adjusted for inflation, have remained stagnant over the past seven years, and personal savings have hit negative levels.

Bush/Cheney created just over 6 million jobs in their first seven years. The previous eight years saw about 23 million new jobs created (Dept. of Labor). Now, many claim that was due to the dot.com boom, which is partially true. Conversely, the twelve years of Reagan/Bush were beneficiaries of the home and business computer boom. One cannot surf without a board. No one had computers in 1980.

So let's be honest. Can we afford more tax cuts? I'm not suggesting tax increases, but surely am suggesting the current cuts should expire rather than be permanent as the Republicans promote. Upon examining their record, they have no credibility on any fiscal matters.

***

(October 2008)

Well, here's another fine mess you've gotten us into. Even Laurel and Hardy can't make this economic situation funny. How in the world did we get here? Let's start with the basics.

First, Capitalism requires competition by definition, and competition needs rules and refs. From card games to football and from golf to debating, every competition is governed by rules and impartial judges, refs, umps, etc.

Second, the Constitution recognizes this basic, simple fact and addresses it in clear language in Article I, Section 8 under the Powers of Congress. Two specific powers are "to regulate Commerce with foreign Nations, and among the several States" and "To coin Money, regulate the Value thereof". That's pretty straight forward. [Definition: regulate - to govern or direct according to rule.]

Third, Article VI of the constitution says, "The Senators and Representatives before mentioned, and the Members of the several State Legislatures, and all executive and judicial Officers, both of the United States and of the several States, shall be bound by Oath or Affirmation, to support this Constitution…." and that oath states the following: "I do solemnly swear (or affirm) that I will support and defend the Constitution of the United States against all enemies, foreign and domestic; that I will bear true faith and allegiance to the same; that I take this obligation freely, without any mental reservation or purpose of evasion; and that I will well and faithfully discharge the duties of the office on which I am about to enter: So help me God."

Our founders recognized that a system based on capitalism

needed rules and refs and clearly made it a priority, its Article I: Powers of Congress, and even developed an oath (Article 6) to ensure that these powers were carried out no matter your ideology. That's what oaths are. One puts ideology aside to "protect and defend the Constitution......against all enemies, foreign **and domestic**" and "faithfully discharge the duties of the office", not faithfully promote ideology that contradicts Constitutional protocol and dictum.

That's how we got here. Blind ideology was allowed to dictate policy, even when that ideology put constitutional officers at odds with their oath and their duties of the office. The ideology basically calls for no rules and no impartial refs. Party ideologues are appointed specifically for their partiality.

Let's go back to the basics and look at that competition thing again. I've witnessed many changes in many competitions over my many years (is that too many manys?). Never have I seen a move to fewer rules and fewer impartial refs. Usually it's just the opposite. Most competitors support the integrity of the competition, but some, mostly those who intend to lie, cheat, and steal, want to denigrate the rules and their enforcement. Those Americans who support the integrity of the free market know and understand the need for rules and refs. Those who don't understand have created a free-for-all market with fewer competitors, fewer rules, and fewer impartial refs.

As a result, the banking system has become even more consolidated and more susceptible to failure because of that fact. If ever rules and refs were needed to ensure that collapse does not occur, it is now. The rescue bill (bailout) must have measures that bring the most basic of constitutional tenets back - that of oversight and full transparency. If it doesn't, get back to work and amend it because this administration has a history of being loose with the truth and less than transparent. Then, a "Ma Bell" type break-up is needed to diffuse future potential calamities.

WE NEED MORE COMPETITORS, not less. Capitalism requires it by definition. Anti-trust and anti-monopoly laws need proper enforcement and need updating to ensure that no industry is dominated by firms "too big to fail". Both Roosevelts knew this and spoke truth to power. It is time again to speak truth to power.

**

(November 2008)

The banks need capital! The banks need capital! Otherwise, they have no money to lend to borrowers, and these borrowers are businesses trying to meet payroll. Without these funds, people will lose jobs. The banks need capital!

So started a bailout totaling nearly one trillion dollars, from a three page demand with no conditions, submitted by Sec. Paulson, to a bi-partisan bill (with caveats) barely passing Congress. It was far from perfect, but supposedly an infusion of direly needed capital for priming the lending pumps. So how's that working?

Well, many recipients of this capital are using it to pay dividends. That's right. Bailout capital, taxpayer money, is being diverted to shareholders. Other recipient institutions are buying up smaller, solvent banks with bailout capital. Buying out lending competitors isn't what we expect. Is it? The purpose was to lend to, "businesses trying to meet payroll. Without these funds, people will lose jobs."

Time and time again, this administration has gamed the system or allowed the gaming of the system, and I'm tired of it. I'm tired of thieves acting with impunity. I'm tired of the deceit and fear-mongering used to achieve these nefarious ends. I'm tired of the false implications and accusations against those who speak out against this travesty. Somebody needs to go to jail. No. Make that many need to go to jail.

Hopefully, full investigations will be part of the change both parties seek, because I have a feeling I'm not alone in my disgust for those who refuse to police the systems they are paid to police. This includes CEO's, Representatives who didn't act when action is demanded by both the public and opposition party members, administration appointees, and most of all, Bush and Cheney. They gamed us the most.

***

(January 2009)

The absolute refusal, by those responsible, to take ownership of the financial collapse clearly demonstrates the even bigger problem America faces in the next few years. These people still control most media outlets and they still have many representatives espousing their failed policies.

George W. Bush enacted the largest tax cuts in history, most which went to the top 1%. The purpose, to create jobs, to invest in America. The reality, investment went into foreign plants and workers. The investment went to further bolster competitors of working Americans. Check the job creation figures during the last eight years, pathetic. The number of jobs in the nation increased by about two percent during Bush's tenure, the smallest growth over any eight-year span in seventy years (Dept. of Labor). Gross domestic product over the last eight years grew at its slowest pace since the Truman administration. Wages were stagnant. These are the results of supply-side doctrine.

The media doesn't let one know that. Instead, it spews the usual handfed trash it receives from its corporate masters. In early September, the White House propaganda wing issued a fact sheet entitled, "American Economy Is Resilient in the Face of Challenges." Less than two weeks later the Treasury was screaming for $750 billion or collapse of the financial system was imminent. The failed supply-side mantra still echoes in the halls of Congress. Tax cuts for everyone, but the consumer, is the conservative cry. We just went through that. It doesn't work, but no will own up to that fact.

***

(February 2009)

The Ronald Reagan tax cuts. The Republicans want stimulus like the Reagan tax cuts. Well, raising taxes isn't the prescription for our troubles. That's right. Reagan raised taxes on most Americans. Only the wealthy benefited.

The self-employment tax was 10.1% in 1980. By the time Reagan left office, it was over 15%. That's nearly a 50% rate increase even before adding on the income tax. The lower income tax rates (0% -14%) were eliminated. The lowest tax rate became 15%. Households making less than the median income, 50% of all households, saw their taxes either rise or remain nearly the same under Reagan. The wealthiest Americans saw the top rate of 70% reduced to 28%, and upper middle class households saw their taxes reduced from 40-48% range to 33% (IRS). That's class warfare people.

Add in the reduction of the capital gains tax, now at 15%, and unbelievably you get millionaires and billionaires paying a lower tax

36

rate than the self-employment tax rate of 15.3%. Again, that hasn't even factored in the income tax rate(s) of 15% - 28% for most self-employed people. This is morally reprehensible. The top corporate tax rate(s) in 1980 were 40-46%. By 1988, those rates had been reduced to 34-39%.

In essence, it places a massive shift in tax burden on lower income people and self-employed people. The added Social Security funds are borrowed "off the books" for a deceptive looking lower deficit - a Ponzi scheme that increases our unfunded liabilities by trillions. That's trillions. Alan Greenspan dreamed up the idea of raising the social security rate for borrowing "off the books". Remember him? He deregulated the banking industry. Thanks Alan. Thanks Mr. Reagan. Please, no more of your tax cuts. I can't afford it.

***

(April 2009)

"Terrorist". "Kill him". "Muslim", yelled some attendees to cheers at McCain/Palin campaign stops. To John McCain's credit, he visibly flinched at the "kill him" scream, and he aggressively grabbed a microphone and corrected a delusional woman defaming Obama. Thank you Sen. McCain. A documentary of the McCain campaign showing supporters brandishing picket signs, asked one supporter "what brings you together here today?" The response, "We all hate the same things". Really.

Many of us thought of these as acts of the fringe, but recent events have proven otherwise. It is painfully obvious that a growing segment of Republicans is driven by hate. I had not heard the term "nigger" for years, but it is commonplace with my Republican acquaintances. McCarthyism is rampant. U.S. Republican represen-tatives have called for an armed revolution against Democrats and the "17 socialists (unnamed of course)" in Congress. It is hate and berate and allow no debate. Call them a name and say they're to blame. Pure hatriotism. No policy debates. Just hate. No solutions. More hate.

Some of us believe the Iraq war was wrong. Where's Bin Laden? Republicans call us a name (unpatriotic). Many of us believe torture is morally reprehensible, but the Christian Republicans defend these horrible acts and call opponents "weak on terrorism" or "supporting terrorism". I wonder what God thinks. When doctors ask us to list our medical history, we hope it is because they want to cure us, not deny us insurance coverage because of broadly defined "pre-existing conditions". Suggesting change in this system is socialism or communism. Keep it the same, Republicans say. Trust the insurance companies. During the Eisenhower years, the top tax rate was over 90%. In 1980, it was near 70%. Now, a proposal to return the top rate from 35% to 39% is income redistribution. It wasn't income redistribution when these top rates were drastically cut, despite the fact that middle and lower income earners have experienced stagnant growth for the three decades since, after three solid decades of income growth, while the wealthiest have experienced record income growth. No. That wasn't income redistribution.

For the last seven years many of us, in this newspaper, warned of burgeoning deficits caused by unwise tax policy. Former Treasury Sec. Paul O'Neill was promptly fired for daring to speak with fiscal sanity. There was no outrage from Republicans. Even as George Bush inherited a record $200+ billion budget surplus and turned it into a record $1.2 trillion budget deficit (CBO) with a broken economy, there was no outrage. Inaugurate a new President and sudden outrage blossoms (tea parties). Where were the tea parties, as $800 billion and counting was put on your children's credit card for the unnecessary war in Iraq? The first U.S. war ever not paid for by tax increases. Where were the tea parties, as $1.2 trillion was put on your children's credit card for tax cuts for millionaires during war time, or the doubling of debt from 2001 to 2009? There was no outrage and no jobs; rather massive job losses unseen since the Great Depression.

How about a tea party against the Republican proposal of cutting top marginal tax rates to 25%, allowing Wall Street thieves to profit even more, or a tea party encouraging more regulation (Article I Section 8) on unregulated mortgage origination? That's right. Mortgage origination is unregulated. They can offer any type of loan, no-doc, stated income, sub-prime, and have without a government edict as claimed by uninformed Republicans. No law required those loans. The Community Reinvestment Act (CRA) does not require those loans as claimed. Here's a statement from the Federal Reserve website: "Neither the CRA nor its implementing regulation gives specific criteria for rating the performance of depository institutions. Rather, the law indicates that the evaluation process should accommodate an institution's individual circumstances. Nor does the law require institutions to make high-risk loans that jeopardize their safety. To the contrary, the law makes it clear that an institution's CRA activities should be undertaken in a safe and sound manner." Who needs facts when there's hate. It's easier to call people names than research and find solutions.

It's too costly to build massive wind farms or solar collectors to wean us from oil/coal. However, continual war costs over resources and on-going costs associated with exploration, drilling, extraction, and distribution, apparently aren't. A wind farm or solar farm will require more initial investment, but far, far less in on-going expenses, not to mention less pollution, less war. Its drill, baby, drill. Trust the oil companies we're told.

So, please Republicans, turn off Fox News. Tune out Rush Limbaugh, Sean Hannity, Bill O'Reilly and Glen Beck. They offer no solutions, none. They decry constitutionally mandated oversight as socialism, tax fairness as income redistribution, energy independence as eco-terrorism, and torture as a tool against terrorism. Please, engage in fair policy debate without calling people names or marginalizing them as commies or socialists. Remember, our armed forces are socialized. Our police force, our fire-fighters, our teachers, our judges, our space program, our food inspectors, our airway controllers, our national parks system are all socialized and for the most part function exceedingly well if properly managed. As a matter of fact, they function better than many private industries, health care specifically. So let's engage in honest, constructive debate and end the hate.

***

(August 2009)

The Bush tax cuts were passed by a Republican congress (Denny Rehberg) and signed by a Republican president with full knowledge of the 'sunset provision' which are legally required if their effect increases future deficits. That means that they did not increase revenues. The CBO and every Bush economic advisor have stated that tax cuts to the wealthy do not increase revenues. Alan Greenspan echoed that same sentiment just recently. Tax cuts do not increase revenues. They cause deficits.

Republican after Republican is still arguing for the extension of tax cuts for the wealthy, even though they will add trillions to the deficits and have been shown to create virtually no new jobs. The premise is that they pay for themselves or increase revenues. Outright lies. These same lies have been told for decades. (i.e. Reaganomics, Voodoo economics, a "Trojan horse" - quote from David Stockman, Reagan Budget Director.)

Denny Rehberg and his "top 1% club" have been wrong and are still wrong. The economy is being cash cowed, taking profits without investing for the future, by Rehberg and his "top 1% club". They will not invest to create jobs in America. They choose China/India. They will not rebuild our infrastructure. They rebuild Iraq/Afghanistan instead, after destroying them. They will not increase pay when productivity increases. They cut pay and benefits.

Yet Rehberg wants to give his "top 1% club" more tax cuts. Apparently the cash cow has not been milked dry enough by corporate America.

***

(November 2009)

"I have not yet heard people in the Republican Party admit they have a problem," Glen Beck told a packed ballroom in Washington. "I have not seen a come-to-Jesus meeting. ... 'Hello, my name is the Republican Party and I've got a problem. I'm addicted to spending and big government'. ... They need that moment."

It's time to own up Republicans. For thirty years, the mantra has been to shovel money at America's wealthiest in the hopes that it would trickle down. Instead, it was voodoo, as per George H.W. Bush. A "Trojan horse", as per David Stockman, Reagan's budget director. During the first eight years of supply-side, the United States went from the world's largest creditor nation to the world's largest debtor nation. Deficit hawks were purged from the Republican Party and replaced by tax cut zombies, whose response to any problem was, "Tax cuts!" During the last nine years and continuing through this year, lavish tax cuts to the wealthiest have not produced the desired outcome, rather they have contributed to enormous deficits. From day one, the current (Obama) administration has been burdened with the costs of paying for non-funded tax cuts, unfunded wars, and unfunded Medicare/drug costs. This has created interest payments of nearly $400 billion a year and lost revenues near the same. That's almost $1 trillion debt per year in outcome of supply-side policy. All charged to our children and our children's children. By any standard, that is an abject failure. Supply-side has failed miserably.

***

(December 2009)

It's time to set the record straight about free market ideology. Conservatives would have one believe that free market equates capitalism. Nothing could be further from the truth. Capitalism, by definition, requires competition which is subject to rules and is overseen by impartial judges refs, officials, umpire, etc. Free market ideology is based on no rules. The biggest and the strongest survive. Competition is crushed through entry barriers into select markets by industry giants who collude and divvy up market share.

The recent financial meltdown demonstrates the danger of non-competitive markets, yet free markets, dominated by firms "too big to fail". Their power and influence is peddled in the halls of Congress through campaign contributions, lobbying, and placement of industry insiders whose loyalty lies with their corporate masters, not the American people, in government positions. In essence, the foxes are put in charge of the hen house.

Americans need to wake up and discern the difference here. Do we want monopolistic industries? Do we want industry oligopolies? Neither of these scenarios promote capitalism, but both are free market. One could argue convincingly that our investment banking system, our energy system, our food processing system, and even our retail systems (Walmart) are all monopolistic and anti-competitive. The insurance industry is exempt from anti-trust law. They can legally price fix, collude, and divide markets to the detriment of the consumer. Is this capitalism?

The answer is no. It is time to end free market ideology and return to capitalism.

***

(April 2010)

I do not recognize today's Republican Party. They live in denial of their proud heritage.

"It is necessary that laws should be passed to prohibit the use of

41

corporate funds directly or indirectly for political purposes; it is still more necessary that such laws should be thoroughly enforced. Corporate expenditures for political purposes, and especially such expenditures by public-service corporations, have supplied one of the principal sources of corruption in our political affairs." – Theodore Roosevelt.

"Corporations have been enthroned and an era of corruption in high places will follow, and the money-power of the country will endeavor to prolong its reign by working upon the prejudices of the people until all wealth is aggregated in few hands and the republic is destroyed." - Abraham Lincoln.

"In the councils of government, we must guard against the acquisition of unwarranted influence, whether sought or unsought, by the military-industrial complex. The potential for the disastrous rise of misplaced power exists and will persist." - Dwight David Eisenhower.

"I hope we shall... crush in its birth the aristocracy of our moneyed corporations, which dare already to challenge our government to a trial of strength and bid defiance to the laws of our country." - Thomas Jefferson.

On Jan. 21, 2010, the US Supreme Court announced a landmark decision establishing for the first time that corporations enjoy the same First Amendment free-speech rights as individuals. In a 5-4 vote, all conservative judges voted yes along partisan lines, ending 100 years of precedent. Sad, very sad.

***

(June 2010)

Some things you just can't figure. Despite a constitutional mandate to "regulate commerce..." and to "coin Money, regulate the Value thereof..." (Article 1 Section 8), the House has allowed a corporate takeover of oversight. Three decades of deregulation by Republicans and corporate Democrats have removed any semblance of rules and allowed industry insiders to do what they do best: lie, cheat, and steal. The proof is in the excuses made my BP, Wall Street, Enron, AIG, et al. To knowingly and willingly deceive is commonplace. It's PR at its worst. Lie and deny, apparently with relative impunity and the results have been catastrophic.

We got accounting scandals (Enron, Worldcom., Sunbeam,

Arthur Anderson, etc.) due to pre-emptive legislation that basically legalized the creative accounting that caused that problem. Insider trading runs amok. Shores are awash in oil because the powerful oil industry convinced legislators that they could self-regulate and clean-up after themselves. We got an unregulated mortgage industry that sold over-priced (bank appraisers determine the value of property), unaffordable homes to uneducated consumers (no-doc and stated income loans) so the industry could meet the demand of Wall Street derivative traders (the derivative market quintupled from 2002 to 2005). We still suffer from the Wall Street meltdown where those multi-hundred-trillion dollar dark markets allow unrestricted bogus ratings from the agencies employed to rate them. And, we got the "Great Recession". Lest we forget, the Bush tax cuts are still in effect, today, so much for supply-side theory. It has failed miserably.

Simply put, when one's belief is that government should be shrunk to a size where one can "drown it in a bathtub" and that industry insiders should be appointed to the government agencies that oversee those industries, this is what one gets. Government does what we ask. Industry insiders serve their corporate masters, operating under just one rule and one rule only - maximize profits. There is absolutely no social responsibility in corporate America today because there is no personal liability. However, some States are currently considering such a clause for incorporation, thus ending the maximize shareholder profits sole purpose of incorporation.

The present corporate paradigm is straightforward Econ 101; **minimize factors of production** which includes: lowering wages, outsourcing jobs to China, etc., cutting back employee benefits, lobbying to loosen environmental standards, tax cuts, tax relief, and lack of transparency. Much of this is achieved through intense lobbying efforts and legislation crafting. Those billions of dollars in campaign contributions aren't bribes resulting in corruption, nope; they're free speech donations by corporate persons.

One can call this economy free market, but don't call it capitalism. Capitalism is rules-based and requires competition, which requires unbiased rules and refs. The free market mantra, the primary cause of our present problems, remains louder than ever. Radical right-wingers are calling for fewer rules and refs, claiming that the situation in which we find ourselves was caused by too much regulation.

Apparently, when Sec. of Treasury Paulson frantically begged Pres. Bush and the Congress to act quickly to save the economy in Sept. of 2008, it was because too many people knew what was happening? The reigns were too tight? This happened suddenly? No! It took years to steal that much money. Now the schizophrenic right is complaining that the BP spill was a result of the Obama administration being too lax in granting permits without proper oversight mechanisms.

What is it? Too many rules or too few rules? Too many unbiased refs or not enough unbiased refs? Should Congress regulate, as constitutionally mandated or should free market liars and thieves self-regulate? Should the government protect us from corporate malfeasance or encourage it through lack of oversight? Should the Federal Reserve be private? Or should it be disbanded, handing over the fiduciary duties to Congress as Article 1 Section 8 states clearly? What part of the Constitution are you for today? And what part do you want changed? The schizophrenia is dizzying.

The same people who cry for jobs support the globalized market that preys on slave labor, pollutes the planet, and routinely gives us tainted, inferior goods. They want higher paying jobs, but dislike unions. They want lower health care costs, but don't want reform. They hate government, but love their Social Security and Medicare. Less government but more services? They complain about corporate influence, but support the notion that corporations are persons and money is speech. They want tax cuts, but when given them in the 2009 stimulus, they complain about new, non-existent tax increases. They want defunding of ACORN because of misuse of funds, but encourage Halliburton, KBR, Blackwater and others who defraud us with regularity to the tune of billions, not paltry millions. Whew!! Stop the merry-go-round.

Lastly, on the Constitution, I share your concern over defending 2nd amendment rights, but where were you when our 4th amendment was gutted and our 1st amendment compromised? With us? Or against us? Really, I just can't figure these people out.

Until you factor in the Limbaugh/Beck/Fox News effect. Then it all makes sense.

***

(September 2009)

Tax cuts for the wealthy? Why? The wealthiest Americans have seen their tax rates cut by two thirds since 1960. The top 20% of Americans own 85% of total net worth and 93% of all financial worth. That's right. The bottom 80% of Americans own just 7% of financial worth (IRS). No wonder the economy is sputtering.

Working Americans have been plagued by over thirty years of income and wealth distribution to the richest Americans, a nearly three-fold increase, while their yearly take stagnated during the same period. Any wonder why consumer debt has increased. Eighty percent of Americans make less while working more to provide the same family necessities as thirty years ago. The same necessities, not more.

So Republicans blame the poor and seek remedy in cutting social security, a contract on every pay stub labeled FICA. They would void a contract with workers to enrich their already wealthy masters. This is utter nonsense and responsible Republicans need to speak out to their leaders (Limbaugh, Beck, and Palin?). Social Security is solvent until 2037. The future shortfalls need to be addressed, but not now. Not by cutting benefits, voiding a contract. During the Reagan years, the answer was to increase payroll taxes. Reagan raised taxes, unbelievers, on workers and the middle class. Simple fact, own up to it.

Currently, corporate America is sitting on $3 trillion in cash and won't invest it. That's three TRILLION, the most in decades. The problem is not lack of capital. There is plenty of unspent capital, but Republicans insist it's not enough and that transferring money from future social security recipients to the wealthy is necessary. That's what Republicans believe and espouse. I hear it every day. And their working, rank and file followers walk lockstep to their own demise.

***

(November 2010)

Congratulations to the Republicans for regaining the house. I have just two words for you as you proceed to govern. Fiscal Atonement.

It is time to pay for the two wars you charged to our children, $1.5+ trillion. It is time to pay for the Medicare/Drug bill giveaway

45

to Big Pharma, $1 trillion. It is time to find offsets for the jobless, unnecessary, tax cuts to the wealthy that you put on the nation's credit card, $1+ trillion. It is time to pay for your massive defense increases, cumulative $1+ trillion. It is time to address spending cuts for your increased interest on your accumulated debt, over $5 trillion added debt under Bush and $150+ billion in yearly interest. It is time to pay for those things that you did not pay for the first time.

To quote your mama grizzly, "Man-up". You complain about the deficit. You lay blame about the deficit, but you did nothing the first time. Will you now? It is time for Fiscal Atonement. You control the House and have two years. Are you going to walk the walk? Or are you going to handcuff Congress with endless partisan investigations of dubious claims. Are you going to govern? Or are you going to carry out your threat to shut the government down? Are you willing to pay for future tax cuts, or charge them again? Are you ready to focus on our problems, rather than the next election? Are you ready for Fiscal Atonement?

***

(November 2010)

Uncertainty. Corporate America says it's not investing in jobs because of uncertainty. They post record profits, buy back stock, and sit on trillions in cash. They still won't invest in growth. Corporate taxes are at their lowest level ever. Corporate contributions to government revenues are just over 7% of total revenues, down from over 25% just decades past (IRS). This places a larger tax burden on the middle class. Congress has passed bills for massive R & D and investment tax credits, retaining capital gains rates, and employment tax credits, but the Senate has filibustered every one. There is still uncertainty.

Let's get to the real reason. Corporations will not invest in jobs because of lack of demand, a certainty. No competent CEO will produce product, just to have it sit in inventory. Even if they are tax free. It is not uncertainty, rather certain reality that concerns business. Consumers are short of cash due to Wall Street impropriety (mortgage fraud), thirty years of stagnant and regressive wage growth, outsourcing of jobs and their tax base, wealth redistribution through tax policy, and increasing energy and health costs. Consumers are cashed out!

A group called Patriotic Millionaires for Fiscal Strength recently argued, ".....to urge you (a letter to President Obama) to stand firm against those who would put politics ahead of their country. .....We don't need more tax cuts, and we understand that cutting our taxes will increase the deficit and the debt burden carried by other taxpayers."

As Warren Buffet recently stated, "The rich are always going to say …… give us more money and we'll go out and spend more and then it will all trickle down to the rest of you. But that has not worked ……, and I hope the American public is catching on."

***

(December 2010)

Now that the election is over, and all the false claims have been levied, it is time to lend some context and simple math to these assertions, specifically the claims about government spending. A good starting point is to establish a historical chart of our economy and government revenues. GDP is the usual tool of measurement of both the economy and the proportion used by government. A fifty year analysis should depict measurable inter-generational trends, and a starting point of 1960 will negate any WWII "hangover" affects. Beginning in 1960 will also provide a relatively benign historical marker. We were arming against the Soviet threat; income distribution wasn't skewed; upper bracket tax rates exceeded 70%; suburbs were expanding; social programs (Medicare did not exist) were new; and debt was manageable. All statistics were taken from easily accessible U.S. agency figures (IRS, CBO, Dept. of Labor), the same base figures used by Wall Street, college educators, conservative and liberal think tanks, and some news organizations.

Note: inflation adjusted GDP growth was relatively stable and just about doubling every ten years from 1950 through 2000, and up to 2006. Then the Bush Recession began to develop and by 2009, GDP took its largest negative drop in seventy years and has grown very slowly since. The Bush Recession caused a one year loss and future legacy of over $600 billion in government revenues. Budget revenue projections of $2.7 trillion exceeded actual revenues of just $2.1 trillion. Each subsequent year will now bear that revenue loss by lowering future projections. That alone contributed to almost half of the $1.2 trillion deficit in Bush's final budget.

In 1960, government spending as a portion of GDP was just

about 19% with small deficits. By 2000, that figure increased to just over 20% with sizeable surpluses. The major variance was the 1980-92 period where the Reagan tax cuts resulted in revenues decreases and huge deficits. Future budgets had to account for this additional required interest spending, and within ten years, a proven 20% of GDP revenue had brought the budget to balance, created 20 million jobs, and paid down debt. In essence, our government operated at just below 20% of GDP for fifty years. Debt accumulated during the 80's and early 90's was being paid by raising revenues through the Deficit Reduction Act of 1993, about one half of one percent above historical levels until the debt was retired.

Then the unwise 2001 and 2003 Bush tax cuts were passed. Treasury Sec. Paul O'Neil was fired for his objections in 2003. By 2004, our revenue base was contributing only 16% of GDP, and when Bush left office it dropped to under 15% of GDP, a huge deviation from historical levels. Extremely irresponsible without spending cuts, extremely irresponsible. Further exacerbating the situation, government spending increased during that time with unfunded wars, increased and unfunded defense spending, growing and compounding debt interest, and an unfunded Medicare/drug bill. That's even more irresponsible, atrocious. The total lack of responsibility for cutting revenues and vastly increasing spending from 2001 to 2006 is unprecedented in American history and is handcuffing future administrations for decades to come. The Bush administration rosy economic predictions at the time did not come to fruition, and the result was even worse than ever imagined. We got the Great Recession and only 1 million jobs created in eight years. Over 20 million jobs were created the previous eight years.

Revenue sources have been dynamic during the post WWII era. There are three major sources of revenue, not just income taxes as conservatives selectively argue. They are income taxes, social taxes or payroll taxes, and business taxes including ad Val Orem taxes. The addition of Medicare in the 60's, and the evolution of Social Security since 1950 is clearly depicted in these revenue sources. What's interesting is who benefits as these payroll taxes are increased.

In 1950, income taxes were 60% of revenues, social taxes were 7% and business taxes were 30%, with 3% other. By 1980, income taxes remained at 60%; social taxes were 30%; and business taxes were 10% of revenues, a clear history of transferring tax liability from business to workers (due to growing social program costs). By 2005, the ratio had become 56% income tax, 37% social tax and only 7% business tax. Currently, upper income taxes and business taxes are at their lowest level in over fifty years although the burden within those groups varies. Claims otherwise are just incorrect. Since only 70% of GDP is consumer spending, including government Medicare payments for individuals, one could argue that business should contribute a proportional share of revenue (30%), rather than further burdening workers and individuals.

Do you see the transfer of liability to labor and individuals from business? Payroll taxes are paid only on the first $105,000 of income. Income tax had remained somewhat stable through 2000, albeit within that portion tax distribution and income distribution changed dramatically. The Bush tax cuts further continued that transfer of tax burden from business to individuals. Purchasers (workers) lost buying power due to that increased tax burden. Plus, increases in energy, education, and health care were further diminishing discretionary income. Then, they were asked to refinance their homes to spend more (mortgage fraud). The airwaves resounded with cheap money ads for refinancing. The system was gamed to gain access to those consumer assets.

Working Americans have every right to be angry. Despite the fact that they shoulder a growing portion of the tax burden, business has not kept their word on sharing the benefits of reduced tax burden through increased pay and job opportunities. Wealthy Americans have not "trickled down" their benefits either. As Warren Buffet recently commented, "The rich are always going to say …… give us more money and we'll go out and spend more and then it will all trickle down to the rest of you. But that has not worked ……, and I hope the American public is catching on." A recent CBO study found that only 30% of all extra income from tax reduction to millionaires is re-invested in our communities. The rest is taken out of the economy through off-shoring into tax havens.

So, if tax revenues are currently below 15% of GDP, and payroll taxes are over 15% of earnings, who's paying less than 15 percent? I hear of stated tax rates for the wealthy and business of 35%, but they certainly don't pay that much due to tax expenditures (deductions). Their contributions to revenues expose that seldom stated fact. Further, workers also pay federal income taxes which reduce the obligations even further on non-workers (investors). Why should the worker's burden be increased through tax inequities? All I hear are complaints from the wealthy and corporate America. The math just doesn't add up, and the statistics prove them in error. Fact: Corporate and personal tax rates for the wealthy have never been lower and the economy has only once been worse, The Great Depression. History's evidence is not on their side, despite their false claims and empty promises.

In conclusion, why haven't workers benefited? First and most importantly, supply-side economics and its supposed effects has failed to fund our government and failed to deliver to the bottom 80% of Americans. Second, globalization and the dominance of huge multinationals who locate in tax free locales have sucked the capital, the jobs, and their tax base right out of this country. More burdens and less opportunity are placed on the middle class at the same time it is collapsing. The income statistics over the last thirty years prove it. Worker's wages have stagnated. There is no relief in sight as long as those who pay the least cause those who make the least to build their infrastructure and fund their defense.

Corporate America's complete lack of appreciation and social/fiscal responsibility for our infrastructure needs are overwhelming. Perhaps it's time to point the criticism where it belongs. Re-aim America. It's time for fair trade policies and an "Economic Patriot Act" to ensure ALL pay and ALL share in America's past efforts and future opportunities. Our problem isn't about socialism and never has been. It's about fairness and responsibility.

***

(January 2011)

Finally, an honest discussion about the effects of tax cuts (i.e. supply-side theory). The recent debate over the extension of the Bush tax cuts brought to light many of the claims and myths about the effectiveness and outcomes of this failed policy.

First and foremost is the claim that tax cuts to the wealthy increase government revenues. Not only is there no empirical evidence to support this claim, every CBO economist, and every chair of the President's Economic Council over the last twenty years has stated just that.

GDP growth increases revenues, and tax cuts reduce revenues with the hope that increasing growth will replace the lost revenue stream. When revenues are measured as a percent of GDP, revenues have decreased historically with every tax cut and GDP growth has not increased beyond historical levels (i.e. deficits -CBO). Also, the very fact that Senate rules dictated the sunset of those tax cuts because of their negative effect on the deficit should further disprove the claim that tax cuts increase revenues. It was a lie, and still is a lie, regardless of what Fox News says now and has claimed for years.

Second is the notion that tax cuts to the wealthy create jobs. Again, there is no empirical evidence to support this claim. As a matter of fact, the evidence argues just the opposite. Dept. of Labor statistics show that combined job creation during Reagan and the Bush's twenty years in office totaled 21.5 million jobs. The eight year Clinton span, after implementation of the 1993 Deficit Reduction Act (tax increase), created 23.1 million jobs (Dept. of Labor). Almost three times as many jobs were created by balancing budgets than under deficit spending (supply-side). The argument that "no poor person has ever created a job" is baseless and ignorant of our proud "rags to riches" heritage. Bill Gates wasn't wealthy when he started Microsoft; Meg Whitman wasn't wealthy when she started E-Bay; Mark Zuckerberg wasn't wealthy when he started Facebook; and Sam Walton wasn't wealthy when he started Walmart. Get the picture? No one denies that it takes capital to grow a business. That is a given, but the notion that only the presently wealthy have ideas and create jobs is nonsense.

Third is the claim that enacted supply-side policy increased GDP growth. Once again, there is no empirical evidence to support this claim. Here are the GDP growth figures since 1960 (CBO):

1961-1964 (John F. Kennedy / Lyndon B. Johnson, Democrat), +4.65%

1965-1968 (Lyndon B. Johnson, Democrat), +5.05%

1969-1972 (Richard Nixon, Republican), +3%

1973-1976 (Richard Nixon / Gerald Ford, Republican), +2.6%

1977-1980 (Jimmy Carter, Democrat), +3.25%

1981-1988 (Ronald Reagan, Republican), +3.4%

1989-1992 (George H. W. Bush, Republican), +2.17%

1993-2000 (Bill Clinton, Democrat), +3.88%

2001-2008 (George W. Bush, Republican), +2.09%

In 2009, Barack Obama inherited the worst GDP growth (-2.9%) since the end of WW II. Supply-side policy was in full effect. If anything, an argument can be made that GDP decreases (historical context) under supply-side policy.

Fourth is the claim tax cuts to the wealthy is the best stimulus for the economy. A recent CBO study, commissioned by George W. Bush, found that tax cuts for the wealthy were the least effective of all eleven stimuli studied, returning only 30 cents for every dollar spent. The other 70% is taken out of the economy and off-shored in tax free accounts (revenue loss) or invested in other countries (i.e. China, Viet Nam, etc.). In essence, tax cuts to the wealthy strengthened our competitors and deprived us of jobs and their tax base. Where is the patriotism in supporting our Communist enemies? To take a tax break, which places more burden on other tax payers, and build our competitors infrastructure, allowing the free transfer of our technology, and contributing to their tax base vs. our own is near treasonous. Why this stands is incomprehensible.

In conclusion, it has been long overdue to have an honest discussion about the supply-side lie that has been propagandized on the populous for the past couple decades. The advent of so called "advocacy journalism", which presents biased ideology in lieu of objective fact-finding, creates a confused electorate unable to distinguish fact from fantasy. And Fox News, sadly, leads that charge.

***

(March 2011)

Oh, those poor, poor billionaires and their corporations. They are the supposed job creators, and they just can't seem to make it here in the good ol' USA. "Taxes are too high", they claim. "Workers make too much money." Apparently the billionaire soup line is full of these poor, despondent job creators. Meanwhile, the Republican Party is ready to address every need of these hapless, shameless, liars, cheaters, and thieves by taking from the poor and middle class and giving to the rich. How Christian is that? What a crock of Fox News lies.

Maybe a quick analysis of their plight is due. Let's start with tax rates for those making over $250,000/yr. Since 1981, their individual tax rate was cut by over 50% and their capital gains rates cut by over 25% (IRS). Meanwhile, working Americans endured tax increases, thanks to the Reagan payroll tax increase. Income distribution since 1981 has seen a 3-fold increase for these poor, poor, billionaires while working people's wages remained stagnant, despite massive productivity increases. Corporate contributions to revenues have decreased to an all-time low since 1981. Never have corporations contributed less to our revenues than presently. Never. Never have tax rates for millionaires been lower. Never.

While the top U.S. corporate tax rate of 35% ranks as one of the world's highest, their tax liabilities are much less, sometimes nothing. This is due to an extraordinary amount of deductions, write-offs, and other accounting tricks allowing them to reduce their tax burden legally.

Job creation from these tax breaks? That went overseas. By 2006, outsourcing accounted for over $1.2 trillion of lost annual wages (CBO). Some economists have predicted another more than 3 million U.S. jobs, and their $125 billion of wages will be outsourced to cheaper labor markets by 2015.

One wouldn't know that, however, if one watches the Fox news lies. One is told that teachers, firemen, nurses, police, road crews, etc. are raping the economy because they simply want to live a middle-class life. They work hard and want the "American Dream", but this apparently burdens corporate America. Just how much burden is that?

Well, here are a few examples (reprinted with permission) from www.payupnow.org/

General Electric made $10.3 billion in 2009, but received a $1.1 billion tax rebate.

Oil giant Exxon paid a lot of taxes on its $45 billion of net income in 2009, but none of it in the United States. The company uses tax havens in the Bahamas, Bermuda, and the Cayman Islands to shelter its earnings from Middle East and African operations.

Forbes states: "Chevron paid $19 billion income tax in 2008. Of this year's taxes, just $200 million were paid in the U.S." That's a 1% tax rate.

Bankster of America: Forbes asked in 2010: "How did Bank of America not pay any taxes on $4.4 billion in income?" The answers are not for the layperson: tax-exempt income, low-income housing credits, losses on foreign subsidiaries, and TARP repayments, all processed through 115 foreign tax havens and transferred to financial statements that were, according to a Bloomberg report, "so delusional that they invite laughter."

Citigroup had 4 quarters of billion-dollar profits in 2010, but paid no taxes. According to Forbes, "With $17.5 billion in future tax deductions and credits on the books...Citi has many tax-free years ahead of it." Citigroup led the Government Accountability Office list with 427 tax haven subsidiaries.

In 2004 the Washington Post revealed that Hewlett-Packard had "deferred taxation on $14.4 billion of foreign earnings, [thus lowering] its effective tax rate from the statutory corporate income tax rate of 35 percent to 12 percent." It's getting worse. According to dailyfinance.com figures, HP's U.S. income tax rate was 4.3% in 2008 and 2.3% in 2009.

Boeing, which just won a $30 billion contract to build 179 airborne tankers, paid no U.S. taxes on over $4 billion of income in 2010. In fact, they got $124 million back from the taxpayers. The New York Times reported in 2005 that AIG had provided 'questionable' tax counseling services to dozens of wealthy individuals trying to shelter hundreds of millions of dollars in profits from federal taxes. Then, after receiving billions of dollars in bailout funds, the company turned around and sued the U.S. government for a $300 million tax refund.

Koch Industries; the poster child of greed and evil. Their ranching operations use federal land for free. Their Georgia-Pacific paper company uses taxpayer-funded logging roads. Their Iowa ethanol plants are highly subsidized by the government. Charles Koch vehemently defends private property rights, but his company used eminent domain to remove Minnesota homeowners who were in the way of his company's new gas pipeline. Meanwhile, the Political Economy Research Institute has listed Koch Industries as one of the nation's top 10 polluters. No wonder they spend tens of millions yearly through the CATO institute, Americans for Prosperity (Tea Party), and other right-wing propagandists to disseminate their lies (on Fox news).

In 2008 Rupert Murdoch's News Corporation (Fox news) had 782 tax haven subsidiaries in 14 countries. CorporateWatch said this allowed the company to pay "astoundingly low taxes."

Bloomberg.com reported that "Merck & Co Inc., the second-largest drug maker in the U.S., last year brought more than $9 billion from abroad without paying any U.S. tax to help finance its acquisition of Schering-Plough Corp." Said Edward D. Kleinbard, a law professor at USC: "Sophisticated U.S. companies are routinely repatriating hundreds of billions of dollars in foreign earnings and paying trivially small U.S. taxes on those repatriations."

Bloomberg.com reported that "The largest drug maker, Pfizer Inc., imported more than $30 billion from offshore in connection with its acquisition of Wyeth last year, while taking steps to minimize the tax hit...Pfizer spokeswoman Joan Campion said the $10 billion tax hit was indeed erased on the income statement because of the accounting treatment."

According to a U.S. Senate subcommittee report, eliminating tax havens could save $100 billion a year. That's a conservative estimate. The IRS calculated that companies and individuals are holding up to $3 trillion in foreign tax havens. Yet they have no money to "create jobs".

Those poor, poor, billionaires. I feel their pain, and hear their lies every day on Fox news. Turn off Fox news and educate yourselves, Republicans. Quit fighting your neighbors by Fox news decree and start focusing your efforts on those who caused this problem, not those who suffer from it.

***

(July 2011)

So this is how we pay for previously unpaid Republican wars (over 1 trillion and counting), previously unpaid Republican tax cuts (over 1.5 trillion and counting), previously unpaid Republican defense increases from 2001 to 2009 (over 1 trillion and counting) and previously unpaid Republican Medicare/big Pharma giveaways (nearing 1 trillion and counting). We raid Social Security benefits and stiff Medicare recipients. This is supposed Republican fiscal responsibility?

Why didn't you pay for these things in 2001; when the first tax cuts were enacted, and Afghanistan was invaded; or in 2003 when the second tax cuts were enacted, and Iraq was invaded; or in 2004 when Republican members were strong armed to accept deficits and "not negotiate" drug prices for the Medicare/Drug bill? This is insanity. Why didn't you pay for these things when you were in charge of the budget? Why?

I'll tell you why. No one would 'buy' the proposed draconian cuts to social programs at that time, so Republicans created a crisis that should not exist just to scare and fear-monger the public into accepting cuts in social programs that they would never have agreed to at the time. It's" starve the beast" ideology that promotes anarchy (drown government in a bathtub – in other words, end government). It promotes the overthrow of our government by corporate interests (Koch brothers, Walton family, Big Oil, Wall Street banksters, etc.) who wish to pay no taxes and provide no public services.

Social Security did not cause our deficit problems, tax cuts and unpaid wars did. Medicare recipients are not defrauding the system and driving up costs, providers and Big Pharma are. Apparently, only the poor and elderly must pay for Republican fiscal irresponsibility and incessant corporate coddling.

***

(July 2011)

The Bush tax cuts. Republicans defend them as revenue producing and job producing (we got neither), and want to give more tax breaks to corporations and millionaires. I hear it every day.

Question: Did our government and economy perform better under the Bush tax cuts which are still in effect or under the Clinton tax rate (1993-2001)? The stock market more than tripled under Clinton rates. It lost value under Bush. The Clinton rates created over 22 million jobs. The Bush rates created only 2 million jobs, leaving our country mired in a job loss spiral only recently stopped. The Clinton rates paid off debt and balanced the budget. The Bush rates tripled our debt, caused insurmountable deficits and created a depression. The Clinton tax rate funded our government at 20% of GDP, near historic levels of 19% GDP, and paid down some

Reagan/Bush deficits. The Bush tax rates fund our government at around 15% (CBO). Revenues have decreased almost 25% from historic levels (1950-2001) under the Bush tax cuts, by design. Government has been purposely defunded by the "starve the beast" ideologues.

In the meantime, Denny Rehberg and fellow Republicans stand in front of the camera and proudly declare we don't have a revenue problem. This is blind denial of reality, complete refusals of factual evidence. This is an ideological constipated tactic of disproven theory pursuit, designed to create a crisis that should not exist. Our economic crisis is a direct result of "starve the beast" ideology.

***

(July 2011)

Would there have been a Civil War if the southern plantation owners had simply said, "But we're the job creators". "We've helped people move from huts into cabins". "These people don't have to hunt and gather anymore."

Well, that's where we sit today. The modern plantations are factories in China, India, Vietnam, etc. The standard of living has increased marginally for most workers on these plantations. True, they've moved from huts to tenement housing. True, they make enough to buy two bowls of rice vs. one. True, a select few, who are willing to implement sweat shop tactics on their own brethren, are paid better than most and can afford a car and a house. In reality, the only beneficiaries are the wealthy plantation owners. They don't have to distribute income based on productivity; they just move their factories to another place where they marginally increase the basic necessities to the poor and the hungry.

Society praises and rewards these people who have so much money, that they could never spend in their life-time, their children's lifetime, and their children's children's lifetime. We give them tax breaks because they are the "job creators". We let them offshore their earnings, taking it out of our economy and depriving our coffers, because they are able to buy politicians with their corporate money. They use right-wing scare tactics to convince the masses that without them, the rest of us would be nothing. They personify greed and evil, just like 160 years ago.

***

(November 2011)

Supply and demand is the most basic economic principle. If you're Republican, this basic principle, these centuries old law of economics, is wrong. Somehow, tax cuts to workers (payroll tax cuts) who spend all the extra money, returning it to the economy, isn't stimulative, but tax cuts to millionaires who hoard that extra money in foreign tax shelters and take it out of the economy is.

This supply-side, ideologically constipated mindset has been factually disproven over and again. In 2001 and 2003, massive tax cuts were given to the wealthy. From 2001 to Jan. 2009, the private sector created only 1.1 million jobs while the public sector created over 2.4 million jobs (Dept. of Labor), the lowest private sector job growth since Hoover. Since the recession officially ended in June 2009, private payrolls have increased by more than 1 million workers, but government payrolls have declined by 493,000. Isn't that good? Isn't that better?

Who needs facts when you've got an engrained ideological mindset. This mindset somehow believes that demand is driven by supply, the exact opposite of the century's old principle. They don't understand that money produces nothing, absolutely nothing. It purchases production (i.e. labor). Labor produces; capital does not. Capital is only a vehicle for purchasing labor, and there is no lack of capital for the purchase of labor. Trillions in capital is readily available for investment in production, but here's the kicker. Why invest and increase unsold inventories, when purchasers don't have the means to buy? Supply and demand.

***

(March 2012)

Facts. Why doesn't the "right" use facts when the discussion of energy is concerned? Gas was over $4 a gallon at this time four years ago, when the Bush/Cheney cabal ruled. Fox News, Rush Limbaugh, and the Republican establishment were all over the fact, the fact, that a world market exists (we have YOU TUBE, you know). But now, apparently, that paradigm has changed. How? Why is it different now?

Refineries in Texas put U.S. refined gas on the world market, and sell it to China, India, and other places of demand. They do not keep it here; they do not serve our market first; they do not even assure that the Keystone pipeline gas will be for American markets. Fact.

I will never understand the blind allegiance to right-wing hearsay, unless I accept the fact that ignorance is bliss. Intellectual curiosity seems not to exist amongst this group. Some of them still believe that Saddam directed 9-11. Some still believe that Iraq had WMD and somehow, with no evidence whatsoever, exported them, wherever. They still believe that tax cuts for the wealthy will solve our economic problems. They still believe that the deficit is a result of spending only, denying the fact that revenues are 25% below historical levels. This, despite the fact that no tax cut was ever paid for under Bush/Cheney, that wars were never paid for under Bush/Cheney, that the Medicare Drug bill was never paid for under Bush/Cheney, and that increased Defense spending was never paid for under Bush/Cheney. Fact. No Republican ever, ever, proposed paying for wars, tax cuts, and Big Pharma giveaways until an opposition party came to power.

We are no longer knee-deep in bullcrap and lies. It is eye level and threatening to drown us. Fact.

SCARERISM AND HATRIOTISM

(September 2003)

In recent weeks, two disturbing poll results have been reported that should raise some red flags. First, close to 70% of Americans believes that Saddam Hussein was responsible for 9/11.

Second, two out of three Americans couldn't name even one Democratic candidate for President. What does this say about our mainstream electronic media? Journalism is the "reporting characterized by a direct presentation of facts". Not one fact has connected Saddam to 9/11 or Al Qaeda. Nothing, Zero, Zilch, nor any WMD's or nukes. Yet these fallacies were, and still are, sold to the American public with little question from the media. This is propaganda, not news. Were debate allowed, perhaps the electronic media wouldn't be so guilty of participating in this ruse about the Iraqi threat perpetrated by the Bush administration. In this debate maybe, just maybe, one or two of the Democratic Presidential candidates could get some recognition. Many sought the press but were given little exposure.

Is this information available elsewhere, absolutely? However, the public owns the airwaves that are used by most Americans for their fact gathering. News producers have an obligation to present more than one side of an issue, and a duty to investigate any repeated unsubstantiated claims over these public airwaves. Perhaps it's time for the public to demand truth in journalism standards, or screen-bottom crawling disclaimers to the effect that opinion rather than fact is being reported.

Believers in "you can fool some of the people all the time" need only repeat sound-bite innuendo from their daily briefing books to these unquestioning reporters and producers and, in time, people believe what they hear, despite the lack of fact behind these assertions. This is dangerous if it runs unchecked. Further consolidation of the media will only exacerbate this already out of control problem.

***

(Summer 2004)

How many warships does Al-Qaeda have? How many submarines? How many fighter planes and bombers does Bin Laden control? Where are the tanks and heavy artillery of the Islamic fascists (and I only use this term in reference)?

To compare the perpetrators of 9/11 to a standing army, air force, and navy of the past regimes of Germany and the Soviet Union is ludicrous. It's outright scarerism. We are not in danger of conquest as were the European nations in the '40's or the Eastern bloc nations of the 1950's and 1960's.

It sickens me to hear this rhetoric used for purely political purposes, especially when it comes from those who argued, and still infer, that Saddam was responsible for 9/11, that Iraq had WMD and that Afghanistan is now a democracy despite overwhelming evidence that the Taliban is revived.

Mr. Bush, Mr. Cheney, and Mr. Rumsfeld have zero credibility. So they sink to the depths used by those they reference. The last bastion of failed leaders is deceit. In the case of this administration, it was the first bastion. We have been deceived about our enemies, about our allies, and about ourselves. The modus-operandi is clear and obvious.

Yes, we have enemies, due to our policies. We are losing the war of ideas because we are not fighting this war. Apparently, we're fighting Hitler and Stalin.

***

(June 2004)

"A country that hides something, is a country afraid of being caught", said President George W. Bush during an April 13, 2004 press conference.

Where do I begin? Should we talk about the reluctance of President Bush to establish a 9-11commission? Or the subsequent delays in release of information, specifically the August 2001 memo? Maybe we should start with VP Cheney's refusal to share accounts of energy meetings with Ken Lay of Enron? How about the overwhelming evidence that Al-Qaida and Saddam were linked in terror? Or the apparent channeling of approval for Halliburton contracts through Cheney's office?

"A country that hides something is a country afraid of being caught".

How about Attorney General Ashcroft refusing Congressional oversight committees requests for copies of legal memos concerning torture? Unprecedented. Never has Congress been denied documents of this sort. Leaked Defense Dept. documents dealing with the legalities of torture and needing approval by Sec. Rumsfeld seems to be difficult to attain. Could someone give a correct figure on the cost of the war in Iraq? Or how much the new 'Drug bill' really costs? Will prescription drugs be cheaper when prices cannot be negotiated? How about pictures of coffins? Correct figures on casualties, whether by enemy fire, friendly fire, or accident? They're all casualties.

Bush's 1970's reserve time seems incomplete; complete it for us, because "a country that hides something is a country afraid of being caught". Please, spare me the shallow, meaningless rhetoric.

***

(January 2006)

Another State of the Union and another dose of scarerism. It's been over four years since 9/11, longer than the entirety of U.S. involvement in WW II. Yet the fear card gets played again. Enough already. We'll always have enemies given our policies. I refuse to spend my days in fear because Bush says so. I refuse to accept we're at war just because we chose invasion and subsequent occupation, and I refuse to accept the erosion of liberty because Bush says it's necessary. Enough scarerism.

FDR stated, "….the only thing we have to fear is fear itself". I suggest everyone read the full text of that speech. Fascinating. He spoke of unscrupulous, visionless, money-changers whose only standard of success is "the falsity of material wealth" (Enron, Worldcom., HCA Inc., Halliburton et al). Add to this Ike's warnings in 1961, "But threats, new in kind or degree, constantly arise. I mention two only…. (1)In the councils of government, we must guard against the acquisition of unwarranted influence, whether sought or unsought, by the military-industrial complex. The potential for the disastrous rise of misplaced power exists and will persist... (2) You and I, and our government -- must avoid the impulse to live only for today, plundering, for our own ease and convenience, the precious resources of tomorrow. We cannot mortgage the material assets of our grandchildren without risking the loss also of their political and spiritual heritage." Again, read the full text.

Recognize the true threats America. The threats as noted above. The threats lie within. This is not something to fear, but rather to confront with the wisdom exuded by the leaders of yore. Listen not to Bush's scarerism about security; rather understand the threat of our democratic process being subverted from within by those who seek "the falsity of material wealth".

***

(February 2006)

More disturbing facts and allegations are emerging from our military and our allies over the use of torture. A recent article from Reuters alleges that European governments were aware of U.S. renditions, often of innocent people, to black spots in Eastern Europe where torture was being outsourced to civilian interrogators. In addition to these allegations, testimony from the court-martial trial (murder reduced to manslaughter) of CWO Lewis Welshofer in Fort Carson, Colorado has further proven the use of torture by civilian interrogators in Iraq.

My first question is, "Who would go into this business (torture) without a market (U.S. government) to sell these skills?" Next, "Can the private sector perform these functions more efficiently than our military? Did the contract go to the lowest bidder?" This is the supposed reason for outsourcing.

Finally, "Who authorizes these contracts?" It surely is not the lowly privates, sergeants, or chief warrant officers (CWO) who've faced prosecution for deeds that mimic those of the civilian interrogators.

The answers to these questions seem obvious when examined as a whole. These are not sporadic anomalies performed by underlings without supervision. This is policy. Policy condoned and endorsed by the highest civilian officials (Rumsfeld, Cheney, et al), policy with no consequences when performed by civilians who are not covered under military jurisdictions, a sorry policy that endangers each and every American's life. History has proven over and again these tactics are ineffective at best and only contribute to the mistreatment of our own.

***

(April 2006)

Testimony from the Katrina disaster has revealed the underlying danger in the far-right vision of government. Victims repeatedly expressed concerns about the competence of FEMA and Homeland Security. Such as why did FEMA spend over $300 million to buy trailer homes that did not meet its own regulations? Why are they still sitting in a field in Hope, Arkansas rather than placing them where they are desperately needed?

The President's response, "...I've asked Chertoff (Homeland Security) to find out. What are you going to do with them? I mean, the taxpayers aren't interested in 11,000 trailers just sitting there. Do something with them. And so I share that sense of frustration when a big government is unable to, you know -- sends wrong signals to taxpayers. But our people are good, hardworking people."

Hey "W", you are big government. It's been that way for over five years, but why be accountable? Just blame big government while praising those in charge. Can you say oxymoron?

Bush's base, the far-right corporatists, has a goal "...to cut government in half in twenty-five years........to get it down to the size where we can drown it in the bathtub", (Grover Norquist). If that statement of intent isn't treasonous, it certainly reeks of anarchy. After all, this is a government of the people, not of market forces.

To achieve their goal, they either starve select programs / agencies of funds, or manage these programs / agencies so poorly (with unqualified cronies or anti-government advocates) that they fail. Interesting. Mismanage select agencies so poorly that they ultimately succumb to the drowning prophecy. So when government fails, they (conservatives) use their own incompetence as the argument that government can never work anyway, so you might as well keep electing them (conservatives) to have less government. The Katrina victims deserve better. America deserves better.

***

(May 2006)

What does one do to someone who withholds information that could save the lives of thousands of innocent victims, someone who believes that their adversaries are bent on the destruction of their long-held beliefs and liberties, and someone who is so predisposed to carry out their mission that all reason is foregone?

What does one do when the mounting evidence seems to prove that attacks on innocent people were unjust and part of a greater plan? When people who wielded power discounted the voices of reason and subjected those who opposed their views to intense, partisan, manufactured, and unfounded criticism, when the followers of these leaders shout down those who question with accusations of treason and abetting the enemy, when any sense of pragmatic analysis is subjected to questions about their patriotism.

Leaders of the world promote their agendas. Whether they are agendas of economic conquest or religious intolerance, leaders of the world will knowingly and willingly deceive to achieve the goals of those who support them. Religious zealots and globalism advocates differ little in their intensity to subject the unwilling to their narrow world views.

At a time when the world seeks tolerant leadership that promotes the gains of all its citizens, we get leadership that promotes hate and mutually assured death. I ask our leaders to lower the rhetoric and raise the compassion. Please.

***

(June 2006)

In a letter published May 30th, [named person] poignantly described the dysfunction of Congress and pleaded with readers to "take it back". Partisans will assume a change of party control will solve this problem. But it won't. Corporatism knows no party lines, albeit far fewer Republicans ever vote against their corporate masters. The problem is private campaign financing that has turned our representatives into full-time fund raisers and part-time public servants. Money buys access. Money buys votes, and money even allows the crafting of legislation by those who benefit. The political paybacks to the big contributors are blatantly obvious. This is not the intent of our founders.

Contact your representatives and insist they support public campaign financing. By supporting public financing, you eliminate wasteful fundraising activities that only benefit those with the monetary resources to influence our representatives. Our elected officials can then use this time to work on behalf of their constituents and are beholden to no one. That's right. They would be beholden to no one, no political favors for contributions. Sounds simple doesn't it.

I know the corporate response will be that there will be a huge cost to fund campaigns publicly. That brings me to solution number two. Mandate that our public airwaves allow certain timeframes for political discourse. The people own the airwaves. Remove the largest cost of campaigns, useless 30 or 60 seconds ads that more often than not offer no meaningful information, and the cost of campaigns becomes very manageable. While addressing the public airwaves, also reinstate the Fairness Doctrine that required broadcasters to give equal time to opposing views. Americans deserve better than the system we have, and the system can be changed by pursuing a few common sense solutions.

***

(January 2007)

Imagine pulling up to a gas pump, filling your tank from a pump with no meter, and driving away with a full tank of unpaid or fractionally paid gas.

This is exactly the state of affairs in Iraq's oil fields. After four years of occupation, oil meters still have not been installed to monitor the true amount of Iraqi oil production and exportation. 'The only reason you wouldn't monitor them is if you don't want anyone else to know how much is going through,' stated an unnamed petroleum executive. Finally, a statement of truth from the oil industry.

People, the thugs and thieves of the oil industry have again demonstrated with clarity their disdain for all things legal. The same people who have closed refineries creating supply deficiencies that increase prices, who have neglected maintenance of Alaskan pipelines causing spills and supply interruptions, who have heavily funded "fake science" about global warming, and who met secretly with VP Cheney in early 2001 to divvy up Iraqi oil upon its theft need to be brought to justice. Swear them in this time when they testify in front of Congress. Republican committee chairs waived the swearing in last appearance and allowed every executive to lie with impunity about their meetings with Cheney.

Remember, Iraqi oil revenues were to fund the war completely, per Paul Wolfowitz - 2002. Every dollar stolen from Iraq indirectly comes out of American taxpayers pockets. It is time to prosecute the thievery and hold oil executives accountable.

***

(February 2007)

In a letter published January 4th, [named person] refers to Democrats as "America-haters" and appeasers. He claims that somehow since the election America is "a dying nation" and "terrorists are cheering America's demise" and that Democrats will "reduce this country to a Third world status". Wow. Talk about hate.

There are numerous reasons to vote for change. First, Iraq had nothing to do with 9/11 and had no ties to Al Qaeda (sources: 9/11 Commission, Senate intelligence committee, Pres. Bush in an August press conference and too many recently retired generals and ex-CIA bureau chiefs to enumerate). Second, Homeland Security is being compromised by non-enforcement of our southern border and Bush's proposal to sell our ports to an Arab nation that funneled money to Al Qaeda. Third, corporate influence on our legislative process has usurped the rights of working Americans. Abramoff and DeLay are shining examples of everything wrong that needs changing. Fourth, the borrow and spend Republicans, none ever voted for the deficit reduction bill of 1993 that produced budget surpluses in the 1990's, are piling up debt while risking economic disaster under the false pretense that somehow tax cuts solve everything. If lower taxes mean increased revenue, then let's not tax anyone. Fifth, and most important, is the total lack of credibility by this administration. The Downing Street Memo of July 2002 proves that "the intelligence was being fixed around the policy" to invade Iraq. Plus, not one person has ever been located who can corroborate that Bush ever served in Alabama as he claims. He went AWOL.

So, [named person] defend the lies of this administration and attack nations fifteen years after the fact, Saddam gassed his people in 1988 with chemicals provided by the U.S. and the complicity of the Reagan administration. Apparently this makes you feel safer. I'd rather pursue Bin Laden.

***

(February 2007)

So the CIA wasn't wrong after all. Dick Cheney's Office of Special Plans, yet another intelligence analysis office, set up at the behest of Mr. Cheney, Mr. Rumsfeld, Mr. Wolfowitz and other signatures of the "The Project for a New American Century", assigned Douglas Feith to rummage through old intelligence (discarded by the CIA as unreliable, unfounded, and the product of sources with no credibility). Naturally Mr. Feith came to conclusions completely opposite from CIA analysts, yet wholly consistent with the goals of "The Project for a New American Century". Unfortunately, the CIA leadership folded to relentless pressure of Mr. Cheney and friends after an unprecedented number of visits by Mr. Cheney. Never had a sitting elected executive ever spent so much time at Langley.

We've also discovered that the aluminum tubes said to be only for a nuclear program use (as proposed by the Bush administration), couldn't even be re-milled for that use. Add to this the admissions in the "Scooter" Libby trial that Time Magazine, the New York Times, and others were fed volumes of misinformation and persuaded to identify Mr. Libby, at his request, as a "low-level bureaucrat". What we end up with is no evidence: of links to 9/11, links to Al-Qaeda, an operational nuclear program, and the ability to attack us with drones in 45 minutes.

Which leads us to the question; would Americans still support the attack of Iraq? Amazingly, my Republican friends insist it was still a wise decision because Saddam gassed his own people. When I tell them that took place in 1988 with raw chemical materials purchased from American companies and with complicity of the Reagan administration, they still defend the invasion. Unbelievable. We'll suffer for decades from the consequences of unprovoked war with Iraq and letting Bin Laden escape.

***

(June 2007)

Last week I read over and again the editorial about "Al-Qaida cares who wins in Iraq". First, what the hell is victory in Iraq? When we defeat the Sunni's? When we defeat the Shia? The Kurds? Supposedly these are the people we are liberating, or is it only Al Qaeda, who were not there, but followed us after we completely dismantled the Iraq army and police force.

Sunni's hate Al Qaeda almost as much as Shia's do and Iraqi's will quickly dispense with Al Qaeda once we quit meddling in their civil war. The vast majority of Iraqis want us to leave, and most say attacking American troops is okay. Even Reagan knew to leave Beirut when it was determined our presence contributed more harm than good. Eisenhower ran in '52 with the promise of ending our involvement in Korea. Remember, Bush pulled troops from Afghanistan to start a war of choice were there was no Al Qaeda. He left the pursuit of Bin Laden and Al-Qaeda to chase phantom WMD that posed no threat whatsoever.

Leave the Iraqi's alone and let them sort it out. It is called self-determination (stay out of civil conflicts) another policy never considered by this administration. Can Iraqi oil prices be any worse than the oligopoly pricing we're experiencing now? Who cares if Iraq nationalizes their oil? It's their oil. It's Venezuela's oil. It's Canada's oil. It's Saudi Arabia's oil. It's Russia's oil. It's Alaska's oil. It's China's oil. And it's U. S. oil. Get it? Iraq's oil is not ours. If you claim it, you do it through thievery.

Will they follow us here? Al Qaeda has no air force, no navy or ships, no tanks or artillery, and no desire or capability to invade the U.S. They are terrorists who do want to extract revenge for our invasion of their holy land, so stated Al-Qaeda leadership on numerous occasions. It is a lot more convenient, more accessible, and much less risky to fight us nearer their home amongst their brethren than to chase us here. Given the lack of defense in favor of offense, who knows how many may be here, enough to cause havoc and death, but surely no threat of invasion.

What about our defenses? While so many are focused on fighting them there, so we don't have to fight them here; our ports were proposed for sale to Arab financiers of Al Qaeda (Dubai); our southern border is open to anyone; and our imports (i.e. Chinese food additives, Central/South American produce, Indian mangoes -

in exchange for nuclear support) are seldom inspected. Balance is needed. It's our defense that's weak not our offense.

Second. Did anyone watch the sickness of the last Republican debate? While most every other candidate endorsed torture to applause and cheers, Sen. McCain, the only person to endure such a fate, boldly stated to a silenced crowd, "We could never gain as much from that torture as we lose in world opinion." His sentiments were echoed by former marine commander Charles Krulak, who commented on McCain's statement, "assertions that 'torture works' may reassure a fearful public, but it is a false security. We don't know what's been gained through this fear-driven program, but we do know the consequences. Those consequences are retaliatory violence." God forgive those who cheer torture. Commander Krulak is one of many former commanders or CIA officials voicing dissent. How many generals have been fired or quit over Iraq? The number is of historical proportions. Never have so many who served, left the service under protest of the civilians (Bush, Cheney, Rumsfeld, et al) running our military. Never. Go figure.

The cold war was fought through containment and engagement. Our enemies had large armies, navies, air forces, and thousands of nuclear missiles pointed at us. Did we invade? Did we occupy? Did we spy on Americans? Did we torture? NO. Only Bush and his cronies resort to the thuggery that is sure to result in massive repercussions.

Oh how I long for the days of Eisenhower; a man so wary of the military industrial complex he warned us of such; a person who admitted wrongs (an endless quagmire in Korea) and ended wars; a general who viewed war as a last resort while nuclear stockpiles were being pointed at us; a field commander who abhorred torture of any kind; a man who talked to his enemies, as well as his friends; one who strongly supported workers and championed the middle-class; one who proudly proposed a progressive tax system where corporations paid their fair share; a man who expected his generation to pay their bills and preserve for their children; a man who communicated to the citizens through reason rather than fear, a true "uniter", not a divider. What happened to the Republicans of Eisenhower? I miss them.

Finally, the voicing of dissent, especially when the silent majority is in dissent, should never be characterized as liberal media reporting. The liberal media reported the non-existent WMD; reported the phantom links to Al-Qaeda; reported the "mushroom cloud" reference (that Tenet took out of three previous speeches but kept creeping back in later speeches); reported that oil would be cheaper as a result of an Iraq invasion; reported that Iraqi oil revenues would pay for the war; reported Rumsfeld and Franks saying only 30,000 troops would be left by the end of 2003. Various independent studies showed a 17:1 ratio of pro-war analysts vs. anti-war analysts on the major news outlets in the lead up to the war, hardly a liberal bias. The major media reported all the falsities straight from the Bush Administration and scared the hell out of us. I don't consider that liberal.

***

(December 2007)

This is not America. This is not the country envisioned by our founders who painstakingly spent years writing a document to ensure our freedoms.

Free speech zones have herded protestors well out of sight. Honest dissent is quietly stifled while hate-filled propaganda is garishly disseminated, so much for our first amendment freedom of assembly and speech. Our public airwaves have become corporate propaganda machines. News? Never, you're getting partisan opinion. Truth is for Buddhists.

Phone records, bank records, internet usage through data mining, and travel records are now being compiled for God knows what purpose, but it's being done. Our fourth amendment protections are gone. Even secret searches are allowed on hearsay evidence under the guise of terrorism.

The FBI is currently spending $1 billion to establish a data base of everyone's physical characteristics. EVERYONE. How do you think they'll get the information? Legally? This Administration has usurped the power of Congress to declare war, or Congress has relinquished it. What citizens get is permanent war against their wishes. Mr. Bush is in the process of signing an agreement to keep our troops in Iraq indefinitely, so much for the duty of Congress to ratify all treaties. If you're Mr. Bush, you just rename it, so it's not a treaty. Just like renaming POW's enemy combatants, so they can be tortured, then, knowingly, destroying the evidence. Under the guise of terrorism, a citizen can be whisked away to an unknown foreign country and be tortured without the right of habeas corpus. [Torture belongs <u>only</u> in the realm of the evildoers, Mr. Bush. Understand?]

This is not America. The United States has been stolen from its rightful owners, the people. Now the big question is do we try to wrest it back? Or do we start over?

AUTHOR'S NOTE: It is beyond moral comprehension that torture even warrants discussion, that the issue is even defended, that God-fearing people endorse such brutally. Worse of all, they lie and deceive about its effectiveness. When we became a nation of torturers, we no longer were "America". The moral authority that we so readily extend in "pre-emptive" war was rendered moot by our lack of human decency required by both our legal base (Geneva) and our secular (crossing religious lines) base. End of discussion.

***

(August 2008)

The General Accounting Office (GAO), probably the most non-political governmental entity, recently testified under oath about their audit (findings) of an investigation into the Iraqi oil dispersion. The testimony was riveting. Yes, CSPAN was riveting, because information was explained under oath. The truth, unfiltered. No FOX. No Limbaugh, just testimony that, if proven false, could land that person in jail.

Here is a synopsis: U. S. forces control ALL Iraqi oil fields, distribution, and ports. There are still NO flow meters installed to measure oil dispersion after five years of occupation. No accounting. The GAO estimates that 30 % of the oil dispersed is on the black market. Under testimony, the GAO said that they did not know where the 30% of black market oil was going, but U.S. intelligence agencies did know.

Did you get that, U.S. intelligence agencies not only know that 30% of Iraqi oil is being diverted to the black market, but they know where it's going. They know where it's going. God Bless America. Our privatized intelligent agencies know where our privatized oil contractors are diverting oil. Please tell Dick Cheney, because he probably doesn't know.

We are witnessing the greatest theft in mankind. Blind ideologues forget that constitutional loyalty trumps party loyalty. So the game goes on.

***

(March 2011)

Ahhh, I see. It's the teachers, firemen, road crews, police, nurses, and other union members who are the problem. My neighbors are the problem? So rants Fox News. Right-wing media recently presented a retirement plan that had accrued a value of $1.3 million for some eastern state teacher. Then they said that taxpayers were paying for this. Whoa. Wait a minute. Remember "fair and balanced"?

Good for the Union if it negotiates a contract on behalf of its members where 15% of contracted compensation, not taxpayer dollars, is put into a retirement account. They are working on behalf of their members. Should a teacher teach for forty-five years and average $35,000 per year, well below the 45 yr. ave. wages of New York City teachers, and have 15% of their own money invested at 6% money market returns, they will now have over $1.2 million in their retirement account. Should state treasurers under fund these accounts to pay for corporate tax cuts, it is not the teacher's fault.

Fox News has framed this debate that honest, open-negotiated contracts, where union members invest their earnings in their retirement is somehow "taxpayer funded retirement". This lie is so manufactured, so inflammatory, it reeks of ideology. "Fair and balanced"? This is right-wing propaganda. Bill O'Reilly talked of violent outbreaks at the Wisconsin protests while showing a video of two opponents pushing and shoving each other. Problem was there were palm trees in the background, a blatant lie. Wisconsin has no palm trees. Hannity has done the same. Beck is just crazy, delusional. These are outright misrepresentations to get Americans to hate other Americans.

How many more of my neighbors, teachers, nurses, liberals, Muslims, public workers, police, firemen, immigrants, etc. will Fox News ask me to hate? How many more?

***

(November 2011)

George W. Bush, 2002 speech at HUD.

"......less than 50 percent of African Americans and Hispanics own homes. That ownership gap signals that something might be wrong in the land of plenty. And we need to do something about it....So I've set this goal for the country. We want 5.5 million more homeowners by 2010 -- million more minority homeowners by 2010."

"...I've asked Congress to fully fund an American Dream down payment fund which will help a low-income family to qualify to buy......This is a program that provides vouchers for first-time home buyers which they can use for down payments and/or mortgage payments."

"...We need more capital in the private markets for first-time, low-income buyers. And I'm proud to report that Fannie Mae has heard the call and, as I understand, it's about $440 billion over a period of time......"

I'm not sure there can be any more convincing argument against the fallacious claims that the Community Reinvestment Act (CRA), Barney Frank, or the Democrats caused the housing crisis. In 2002, the Congress was Republican controlled, as it had been for eight years and was to be for another four years. George W. Bush and his party passed no laws to address mortgage fraud; rather they implemented new laws to aid minority housing sales. The CRA did not require no-doc and stated income loans as claimed, or they'd still be available today.

Newt Gingrich advocated Bush's homeownership policy as a lobbyist for Freddie/Fannie from 2003 (just after the Bush Home Ownership speech) until the eve of the economic collapse. Even Rep. Bachman has stated, "...he took money to also influence senior Republicans to be favorable toward Fannie and Freddie."

For once, check the facts, Republicans. Read Bush's full speech and check Gingrich's lobbying. Republicans promoted Fannie and Freddie.

GROWING UP MIDDLE CLASS

Though born in Grand Rapids, Minnesota, I was raised in St. Peter, Minnesota. My earliest recollections begin in the late 1950's and early 1960's. We lived then on Front Street, not far from the Minnesota River. My father was beginning what would be a long career with an electronics company, ADC (it was sold multiple times during the 80's with pension raids of retirement funds). My mother was raising the five of us boys, with another on the way. We were the burgeoning middle-class personified.

I began grade school and went to my first Sunday school classes while living on Front Street. First Lutheran Church and Washington Elementary School were within blocks of our house. These were my homes away from home, where I expanded my little world. Our humble church was of 19th century architecture with a beautiful steeple and the most magnificent stained glass windows I've ever seen. My brothers and I attended Sunday school in the addition. My beliefs were spawned there, under the tutelage of Pastor Ahlstrom, one of the most kind and thoughtful humans ever to grace the earth. He taught the lessons of Christianity, rather than the glorification of Jesus. I loved going to Sunday school, but then one day, sadly, the church burned down. I'll never forget it and always cherish it with the fondest memories of innocent youth. I miss that church.

The small town of St. Peter was like so many others of the time, yet it had its own identity. Most every business was locally owned. If you wanted shoes, you went to Burch's. If you wanted men's clothing, you went to Nutter's. If you wanted women's clothes, you went to Bunde's. There were three local drug stores, one with a soda fountain. Box stores and strip malls did not exist. St. Peter declined a Hwy 169 bypass with the stated purpose of keeping traffic for local business. The leaded gas fumes of the increased daily traffic were of no concern, despite the growing knowledge of its deadly effects.

Our city hall, police station, and garbage dump were all located next to the river. I especially loved going to the dump. It was a meeting place of sorts, and even had a pond stocked with fish for the youngsters. While I fished there, the garbage was bulldozed into piles and burned. Then it was bulldozed into the river, just upstream from where the storm sewers emptied into the water. Up and down most every river community, this is how things were done in Minnesota in the early 60's. It was polluting, but it was cheap.

The river bottoms were a massive mosquito nursery after the spring flooding. To combat the hordes, a city truck and trailer, with a generator and large blue-nozzled sprayer, dispensed DDT in plumes in front our house. We would run up and down the street behind the sprayer with nary a care in the world. We knew no better.

In late 1961, we moved to our new house on Upper Johnson, on the other side of town. Rising wages and shared prosperity allowed many single income families to build or buy homes. My youngest brother Rick was born soon after the move and our clan of six boys was complete. Dad was closer to work, but we were farther from school. This kept Mom busy, taxiing us to and fro. The new school, Lincoln Elementary, was next to the community swimming pool and the recreation field where I would spend all my free time for the next half dozen years. The "rec" was a place of childhood dreams. Our teachers and coaches staffed it each summer. We had T-ball, baseball, archery, four square and tetherball. There were two basketball courts, one with eight-foot baskets. In front of the adult pool (there was a wading pool for kids) was a vacant area for pick-up football games.

If we chose, a morning and afternoon bus would take us to and from the golf course, just outside of town. It was nirvana, all provided by a caring community where businesses paid taxes that benefited the family, and family provided labor that benefitted businesses. Family mattered more than profit. My childhood was as good as it got, and Mom and Dad ensured that we were never in need. St. Peter was "Pleasantville" without any falseness or fakery.

My pre-teen years introduced me to new schools, new churches, and new friends. First Lutheran church was rebuilt just blocks from our new home. I could walk to Sunday school and confirmation classes. [In the interim, we attended church at the Chapel on the campus of Gustavus Adolphus College.] Pastor Ahlstrom continued to teach confirmation and schedule us for acolyte duty, which I treasured because it gave me time to talk with him one on one. He was everyone's second father, and he liked it that way. He was so cool. One confirmation class was interrupted for a performance. We were introduced to John Denver. He sang "Leaving on a Jet Plane" to a dozen of us in the church basement meeting room before departing to New York to record his first solo album. His wife to be, Annie Martel, was from St. Peter. She was a friend of Pastor Ahlstrom's sons. The song was about leaving her. How cool is that! (A few years later, John Denver sang at our high school prom.)

Technology brought the world to us in living color, unlike newspapers. The assassinations of President Kennedy, Bobby Kennedy, and Martin Luther King, the war in Vietnam, the protests of that war, and the riots during the Civil Rights movement were broadcast into our homes and autos. St. Peter seemed so far away and safe. As a paperboy, I'd read the headlines and details and wonder every day "what is the world like outside of St. Peter?" It's as if I was atop the bleachers watching it all happen somewhere else. That changed as I became more aware of how these events could affect my future, specifically, the draft.

Had it not been for my love of sports and the outdoors I would have gone crazy worrying about a certain future in Vietnam. My parents excelled at providing me outlets to achieve my needs. They strapped a fiberglass pole to the family station wagon, driving me to regional track meets where I could pole vault. They taxied me from school after football practice or games, offering encouragement at every corner. My neighborhood friend, John, asked me to attend my first Minnesota Vikings game in October of 1968. We'd played football together for years, and his father was my 7th grade English teacher. His mother suffered from polio, so we were allowed to use the service elevator to access our seats. There was no American with Disabilities Act in 1968. As we waited, a limousine and accompanying cars swiftly pulled up. Out stepped Vice President

Hubert Humphrey, flanked by a cadre of Secret Service agents. They, too, needed to use the service elevator so Presidential candidate Humphrey could access his seats. In retrospect it seems surreal. The assassinations of Bobby Kennedy and Martin Luther King had occurred just months prior, yet I was unexpectedly occupying an elevator with a man who could be our next President. He engaged in conversation immediately, asking our names. We talked football. His manner was friendly and neighborly, as if we'd known each other for years. I can see now why he was a politician. We reached our level and said goodbye. His smile was genuine. The Vikings lost to the Rams. Humphrey lost to Nixon.

My dad took me camping in the boundary waters canoe area for a week in July of 1969, sort of a rite of passage. My friend, Randy, and his father joined us. We portaged three times. A week in the wilderness and I caught the biggest fish of my life. It bent the landing net. We listened "live" to Neil Armstrong's "one small step..." on a transistor radio as we sat under the full moon next to the campfire at the islands edge while eating pan-fried walleye. In retrospect, that moment also seems surreal. These outlets simultaneously provided me distraction and engagement in events waiting to engulf me. The world was coming to me.

Many of my friends had older brothers. The more time I spent with them the more I grew to dislike war. First I heard of their friends getting drafted, and then they were. Some came home without limbs, some in a box, and some not at all. The war was touching my friends and me with the stark reality of perhaps getting drafted. No one ever adequately explained why teenage boys were sent off to fight a war of dubious purpose. They just did it, and I didn't like what it did to the families required to sacrifice. There was no morality in what seemed an endless campaign against an ideological mindset. We killed commies because they were commies, or were about to become commies. (Yet today Communist China is embraced because they offer slave labor and no environmental regulations.) It all seemed senseless, and I had no choice. By 1970, there were no draft deferments of any kind. I feared the draft every day through my teenage years.

By the early 1970's, much had changed. The city wasn't openly spraying DDT or disposing burned trash into the river thanks to the environmental movement and the subsequent creation of the EPA

(1969). Walter Cronkite and the independent media had declared the Vietnam War a lost cause, much to the chagrin of the military/industrial complex. Medicare had been created to fill the gap the insurance industry was reluctant to cover. Civil rights legislation was enacted. Schools and the workplace were integrated. Employment discrimination of women was legislatively addressed, but not without resistance. Eighteen year olds, who were required to fight for their country, could now vote. The hippie movement, free love, long hair and communes were manifestations against those who promoted war, segregation, and pollution.

As polluted rivers burned, as Lake Eire became fishless, as major cities endured increased smog alerts, as anti-war protests grew, and as unarmed student protestors were murdered by our own troops in 1970 at Kent State University, an angry class of industrialists counter-rebelled and began to put into place their roadmap for future control. They felt they could pollute and discriminate, and even felt the murders at Kent State were justified. In a statement of utter disbelief, then Gov. Ronald Reagan of California said about the killings, "If there's to be a bloodbath, let it be now." His quote captured corporate sentiment, and he quickly became their leader, elected President in 1980. At a time when these industrialists could have sought resolution of common problems, they sought to vanquish their enemies instead. No longer would corporations answer to EEOC requirements, EPA requirements, Unions, and a free press. And we've suffered for it ever since, at the expense of the largest middle-class the world has ever known, the largest middle-class that, sadly, no longer exists.

Thanks to the supply-side lie.

THE POWELL MEMO

Reprinted with permission from
http://www.reclaimdemocracy.org/
corporate_accountability/powell_memo_lewis.html

DATE: August 23, 1971

TO: Mr. Eugene B. Sydnor, Jr., Chairman, Education Committee, U.S. Chamber of Commerce

FROM: Lewis F. Powell, Jr.

This memorandum is submitted at your request as a basis for the discussion on August 24 with Mr. Booth (executive vice president) and others at the U.S. Chamber of Commerce. The purpose is to identify the problem, and suggest possible avenues of action for further consideration.

Dimensions of the Attack

No thoughtful person can question that the American economic system is under broad attack.1 This varies in scope, intensity, in the techniques employed, and in the level of visibility.

There always have been some who opposed the American system, and preferred socialism or some form of statism (communism or fascism). Also, there always have been critics of the system, whose criticism has been wholesome and constructive so long as the objective was to improve rather than to subvert or destroy.

But what now concerns us is quite new in the history of America. We are not dealing with sporadic or isolated attacks from a relatively few extremists or even from the minority socialist cadre. Rather, the assault on the enterprise system is broadly based and consistently pursued. It is gaining momentum and converts.

Sources of the Attack

The sources are varied and diffused. They include, not unexpectedly, the Communists, New Leftists and other revolutionaries who would destroy the entire system, both political and economic. These extremists of the left are far more numerous, better financed, and increasingly are more welcomed and encouraged by other elements of society, than ever before in our history. But they remain a small minority, and are not yet the principal cause for concern.

The most disquieting voices joining the chorus of criticism come from perfectly respectable elements of society: from the college campus, the pulpit, the media, the intellectual and literary journals, the arts and sciences, and from politicians. In most of these groups the movement against the system is participated in only by minorities. Yet, these often are the most articulate, the most vocal, the most prolific in their writing and speaking.

Moreover, much of the media-for varying motives and in varying degrees-either voluntarily accords unique publicity to these "attackers," or at least allows them to exploit the media for their purposes. This is especially true of television, which now plays such a predominant role in shaping the thinking, attitudes and emotions of our people.

One of the bewildering paradoxes of our time is the extent to which the enterprise system tolerates, if not participates in, its own destruction.

The campuses from which much of the criticism emanates are supported by (i) tax funds generated largely from American business, and (ii) contributions from capital funds controlled or generated by American business. The boards of trustees of our universities overwhelmingly are composed of men and women who are leaders in the system.

Most of the media, including the national TV systems, are owned and theoretically controlled by corporations which depend upon profits, and the enterprise system to survive.

Tone of the Attack

This memorandum is not the place to document in detail the tone, character, or intensity of the attack. The following quotations will suffice to give one a general idea:

William Kunstler, warmly welcomed on campuses and listed in a recent student poll as the "American lawyer most admired," incites audiences as follows:

"You must learn to fight in the streets, to revolt, to shoot guns. We will learn to do all of the things that property owners fear."2 The New Leftists who heed Kunstler's advice increasingly are beginning to act -- not just against military recruiting offices and manufacturers of munitions, but against a variety of businesses: "Since February, 1970, branches (of Bank of America) have been attacked 39 times, 22 times with explosive devices and 17 times with fire bombs or by arsonists."3 Although New Leftist spokesmen are succeeding in radicalizing thousands of the young, the greater cause for concern is the hostility of respectable liberals and social reformers. It is the sum total of their views and influence which could indeed fatally weaken or destroy the system.

A chilling description of what is being taught on many of our campuses was written by Stewart Alsop:

"Yale, like every other major college, is graduating scores of bright young men who are practitioners of 'the politics of despair.' These young men despise the American political and economic system . . . (their) minds seem to be wholly closed. They live, not by rational discussion, but by mindless slogans."4 A recent poll of students on 12 representative campuses reported that: "Almost half the students favored socialization of basic U.S. industries."5

A visiting professor from England at Rockford College gave a series of lectures entitled "The Ideological War Against Western Society," in which he documents the extent to which members of the intellectual community are waging ideological warfare against the enterprise system and the values of western society.

In a foreword to these lectures, famed Dr. Milton Friedman of Chicago warned: "It (is) crystal clear that the foundations of our free society are under wide-ranging and powerful attack -- not by Communist or any other conspiracy but by misguided individuals parroting one another and unwittingly serving ends they would never intentionally promote."6

Perhaps the single most effective antagonist of American business is Ralph Nader, who -- thanks largely to the media -- has become a legend in his own time and an idol of millions of Americans. A recent article in Fortune speaks of Nader as follows:

"The passion that rules in him -- and he is a passionate man -- is aimed at smashing utterly the target of his hatred, which is corporate power. He thinks, and says quite bluntly, that a great many corporate executives belong in prison -- for defrauding the consumer with shoddy merchandise, poisoning the food supply with chemical additives, and willfully manufacturing unsafe products that will maim or kill the buyer. He emphasizes that he is not talking just about 'fly-by-night hucksters' but the top management of blue chip business."7

A frontal assault was made on our government, our system of justice, and the free enterprise system by Yale Professor Charles Reich in his widely publicized book: "The Greening of America," published last winter.

The foregoing references illustrate the broad, shotgun attack on the system itself. There are countless examples of rifle shots which undermine confidence and confuse the public. Favorite current targets are proposals for tax incentives through changes in depreciation rates and investment credits. These are usually described in the media as "tax breaks," "loop holes" or "tax benefits" for the benefit of business. * As viewed by a columnist in the Post, such tax measures would benefit "only the rich, the owners of big companies."8

It is dismaying that many politicians make the same argument that tax measures of this kind benefit only "business," without benefit to "the poor." The fact that this is either political demagoguery or economic illiteracy is of slight comfort. This setting of the "rich" against the "poor," of business against the people, is the cheapest and most dangerous kind of politics.

The Apathy and Default of Business

What has been the response of business to this massive assault upon its fundamental economics, upon its philosophy, upon its right to continue to manage its own affairs, and indeed upon its integrity?

The painfully sad truth is that business, including the boards of directors' and the top executives of corporations great and small and business organizations at all levels, often have responded -- if at all -- by appeasement, ineptitude and ignoring the problem. There are, of course, many exceptions to this sweeping generalization. But the net effect of such response as has been made is scarcely visible.

In all fairness, it must be recognized that businessmen have not been trained or equipped to conduct guerrilla warfare with those who propagandize against the system, seeking insidiously and constantly to sabotage it. The traditional role of business executives has been to manage, to produce, to sell, to create jobs, to make profits, to improve the standard of living, to be community leaders, to serve on charitable and educational boards, and generally to be good citizens. They have performed these tasks very well indeed.

But they have shown little stomach for hard-nose contest with their critics, and little skill in effective intellectual and philosophical debate.

A column recently carried by the Wall Street Journal was entitled: "Memo to GM: Why Not Fight Back?"9 Although addressed to GM by name, the article was a warning to all American business. Columnist St. John said:

"General Motors, like American business in general, is 'plainly in trouble' because intellectual bromides have been substituted for a sound intellectual exposition of its point of view." Mr. St. John then commented on the tendency of business leaders to compromise with and appease critics. He cited the concessions which Nader wins from management, and spoke of "the fallacious view many businessmen take toward their critics." He drew a parallel to the mistaken tactics of many college administrators: "College administrators learned too late that such appeasement serves to destroy free speech, academic freedom and genuine scholarship. One campus radical demand was conceded by university heads only to be followed by a fresh crop which soon escalated to what amounted to a demand for outright surrender."

One need not agree entirely with Mr. St. John's analysis. But most observers of the American scene will agree that the essence of his message is sound. American business "plainly in trouble"; the response to the wide range of critics has been ineffective, and has included appeasement; the time has come -- indeed, it is long overdue -- for the wisdom, ingenuity and resources of American business to be marshalled against those who would destroy it.

Responsibility of Business Executives

What specifically should be done? The first essential -- a prerequisite to any effective action -- is for businessmen to confront this problem as a primary responsibility of corporate management.

The overriding first need is for businessmen to recognize that the ultimate issue may be survival -- survival of what we call the free enterprise system, and all that this means for the strength and prosperity of America and the freedom of our people.

The day is long past when the chief executive officer of a major corporation discharges his responsibility by maintaining a satisfactory growth of profits, with due regard to the corporation's public and social responsibilities. If our system is to survive, top management must be equally concerned with protecting and preserving the system itself.

This involves far more than an increased emphasis on "public relations" or "governmental affairs" -- two areas in which corporations long have invested substantial sums.

A significant first step by individual corporations could well be the designation of an executive vice president (ranking with other executive VP's) whose responsibility is to counter-on the broadest front-the attack on the enterprise system. The public relations department could be one of the foundations assigned to this executive, but his responsibilities should encompass some of the types of activities referred to subsequently in this memorandum. His budget and staff should be adequate to the task.

Possible Role of the Chamber of Commerce

But independent and uncoordinated activity by individual corporations, as important as this is, will not be sufficient. Strength lies in organization, in careful long-range planning and implementation, in consistency of action over an indefinite period of years, in the scale of financing available only through joint effort, and in the political power available only through united action and national organizations.

Moreover, there is the quite understandable reluctance on the part of any one corporation to get too far out in front and to make itself too visible a target.

The role of the National Chamber of Commerce is therefore vital. Other national organizations (especially those of various industrial and commercial groups) should join in the effort, but no other organizations appear to be as well situated as the Chamber. It enjoys a strategic position, with a fine reputation and a broad base of support. Also -- and this is of immeasurable merit -- there are hundreds of local Chambers of Commerce which can play a vital supportive role.

It hardly need be said that before embarking upon any program, the Chamber should study and analyze possible courses of action and activities, weighing risks against probable effectiveness and feasibility of each.

Considerations of cost, the assurance of financial and other support from members, adequacy of staffing and similar problems will all require the most thoughtful consideration.

The Campus

The assault on the enterprise system was not mounted in a few months. It has gradually evolved over the past two decades, barely perceptible in its origins and benefiting (sic) from a gradualism that provoked little awareness much less any real reaction.

Although origins, sources and causes are complex and interrelated, and obviously difficult to identify without careful qualification, there is reason to believe that the campus is the single most dynamic source. The social science faculties usually include members who are unsympathetic to the enterprise system. They may range from a Herbert Marcuse, Marxist faculty member at the University of California at San Diego, and convinced socialists, to the ambivalent liberal critic who finds more to condemn than to commend. Such faculty members need not be in a majority. They are often personally attractive and magnetic; they are stimulating teachers, and their controversy attracts student following; they are prolific writers and lecturers; they author many of the textbooks, and they exert enormous influence -- far out of proportion to their numbers -- on their colleagues and in the academic world.

Social science faculties (the political scientist, economist, sociologist and many of the historians) tend to be liberally oriented, even when leftists are not present. This is not a criticism per se, as the need for liberal thought is essential to a balanced viewpoint. The difficulty is that "balance" is conspicuous by its absence on many campuses, with relatively few members being of conservatives or moderate persuasion and even the relatively few often being less articulate and aggressive than their crusading colleagues.

This situation extending back many years and with the imbalance gradually worsening, has had an enormous impact on millions of young American students. In an article in Barron's Weekly, seeking an answer to why so many young people are disaffected even to the point of being revolutionaries, it was said: "Because they were taught that way."10 Or, as noted by columnist Stewart Alsop, writing about his alma mater: "Yale, like every other major college, is graduating scores' of bright young men ... who despise the American political and economic system."

As these "bright young men," from campuses across the country, seek opportunities to change a system which they have been taught to distrust -- if not, indeed "despise" -- they seek employment in the centers of the real power and influence in our country, namely: (i) with the news media, especially television; (ii) in government, as "staffers" and consultants at various levels; (iii) in elective politics; (iv) as lecturers and writers, and (v) on the faculties at various levels of education.

Many do enter the enterprise system -- in business and the professions -- and for the most part they quickly discover the fallacies of what they have been taught. But those who eschew the mainstream of the system often remain in key positions of influence where they mold public opinion and often shape governmental action. In many instances, these "intellectuals" end up in regulatory agencies or governmental departments with large authority over the business system they do not believe in.

If the foregoing analysis is approximately sound, a priority task of business -- and organizations such as the Chamber -- is to address the campus origin of this hostility. Few things are more sanctified in American life than academic freedom. It would be fatal to attack this as a principle. But if academic freedom is to retain the qualities of "openness," "fairness" and "balance" -- which are essential to its intellectual significance -- there is a great opportunity for constructive action. The thrust of such action must be to restore the qualities just mentioned to the academic communities.

What Can Be Done About the Campus

The ultimate responsibility for intellectual integrity on the campus must remain on the administrations and faculties of our colleges and universities. But organizations such as the Chamber can assist and activate constructive change in many ways, including the following:

Staff of Scholars

The Chamber should consider establishing a staff of highly qualified scholars in the social sciences who do believe in the system. It should include several of national reputation whose authorship would be widely respected -- even when disagreed with.

Staff of Speakers

There also should be a staff of speakers of the highest competency. These might include the scholars, and certainly those who speak for the Chamber would have to articulate the product of the scholars.

Speaker's Bureau

In addition to full-time staff personnel, the Chamber should have a Speaker's Bureau which should include the ablest and most effective advocates from the top echelons of American business.

Evaluation of Textbooks

The staff of scholars (or preferably a panel of independent scholars) should evaluate social science textbooks, especially in economics, political science and sociology. This should be a continuing program.

The objective of such evaluation should be oriented toward restoring the balance essential to genuine academic freedom. This would include assurance of fair and factual treatment of our system of government and our enterprise system, its accomplishments, its basic relationship to individual rights and freedoms, and comparisons with the systems of socialism, fascism and communism. Most of the existing textbooks have some sort of comparisons, but many are superficial, biased and unfair.

We have seen the civil rights movement insist on re-writing many of the textbooks in our universities and schools. The labor unions likewise insist that textbooks be fair to the viewpoints of organized labor. Other interested citizens groups have not hesitated to review, analyze and criticize textbooks and teaching materials. In a democratic society, this can be a constructive process and should be regarded as an aid to genuine academic freedom and not as an intrusion upon it.

If the authors, publishers and users of textbooks know that they will be subjected -- honestly, fairly and thoroughly -- to review and critique by eminent scholars who believe in the American system, a return to a more rational balance can be expected.

Equal Time on the Campus

The Chamber should insist upon equal time on the college speaking circuit. The FBI publishes each year a list of speeches made on college campuses by avowed Communists. The number in 1970 exceeded 100. There were, of course, many hundreds of appearances by leftists and ultra liberals who urge the types of viewpoints indicated earlier in this memorandum. There was no corresponding representation of American business, or indeed by individuals or organizations who appeared in support of the American system of government and business.

Every campus has its formal and informal groups which invite speakers. Each law school does the same thing. Many universities and colleges officially sponsor lecture and speaking programs. We all know the inadequacy of the representation of business in the programs.

It will be said that few invitations would be extended to Chamber speakers.11 This undoubtedly would be true unless the Chamber aggressively insisted upon the right to be heard -- in effect, insisted upon "equal time." University administrators and the great majority of student groups and committees would not welcome being put in the position publicly of refusing a forum to diverse views, indeed, this is the classic excuse for allowing Communists to speak.

The two essential ingredients are (i) to have attractive, articulate and well-informed speakers; and (ii) to exert whatever degree of pressure -- publicly and privately -- may be necessary to assure opportunities to speak. The objective always must be to inform and enlighten, and not merely to propagandize.

Balancing of Faculties

Perhaps the most fundamental problem is the imbalance of many faculties. Correcting this is indeed a long-range and difficult project. Yet, it should be undertaken as a part of an overall program. This would mean the urging of the need for faculty balance upon university administrators and boards of trustees.

The methods to be employed require careful thought, and the obvious pitfalls must be avoided. Improper pressure would be counterproductive. But the basic concepts of balance, fairness and truth are difficult to resist, if properly presented to boards of trustees, by writing and speaking, and by appeals to alumni associations and groups.

This is a long road and not one for the fainthearted. But if pursued with integrity and conviction it could lead to a strengthening of both academic freedom on the campus and of the values which have made America the most productive of all societies.

Graduate Schools of Business

The Chamber should enjoy a particular rapport with the increasingly influential graduate schools of business. Much that has been suggested above applies to such schools. Should not the Chamber also request specific courses in such schools dealing with the entire scope of the problem addressed by this memorandum? This is now essential training for the executives of the future.

Secondary Education

While the first priority should be at the college level, the trends mentioned above are increasingly evidenced in the high schools. Action programs, tailored to the high schools and similar to those mentioned, should be considered. The implementation thereof could become a major program for local chambers of commerce, although the control and direction -- especially the quality control -- should be retained by the National Chamber.

What Can Be Done About the Public?

Reaching the campus and the secondary schools is vital for the long-term. Reaching the public generally may be more important for the shorter term. The first essential is to establish the staffs of eminent scholars, writers and speakers, who will do the thinking, the analysis, the writing and the speaking. It will also be essential to have staff personnel who are thoroughly familiar with the media, and how most effectively to communicate with the public. Among the more obvious means are the following:

Television

The national television networks should be monitored in the same way that textbooks should be kept under constant surveillance. This applies not merely to so-called educational programs (such as "Selling of the Pentagon"), but to the daily "news analysis" which so often includes the most insidious type of criticism of the enterprise system.12 Whether this criticism results from hostility or economic ignorance, the result is the gradual erosion of confidence in "business" and free enterprise.

This monitoring, to be effective, would require constant examination of the texts of adequate samples of programs. Complaints -- to the media and to the Federal Communications Commission -- should be made promptly and strongly when programs are unfair or inaccurate. Equal time should be demanded when appropriate. Effort should be made to see that the forum-type programs (the Today Show, Meet the Press, etc.) afford at least as much opportunity for supporters of the American system to participate as these programs do for those who attack it.

Other Media

Radio and the press are also important, and every available means should be employed to challenge and refute unfair attacks, as well as to present the affirmative case through these media.

The Scholarly Journals

It is especially important for the Chamber's "faculty of scholars" to publish. One of the keys to the success of the liberal and leftist faculty members has been their passion for "publication" and "lecturing." A similar passion must exist among the Chamber's scholars.

Incentives might be devised to induce more "publishing" by independent scholars who do believe in the system.

There should be a fairly steady flow of scholarly articles presented to a broad spectrum of magazines and periodicals -- ranging from the popular magazines (Life, Look, Reader's Digest, etc.) to the more intellectual ones (Atlantic, Harper's, Saturday Review, New York, etc.)13 and to the various professional journals.

Books, Paperbacks and Pamphlets

The news stands -- at airports, drugstores, and elsewhere -- are filled with paperbacks and pamphlets advocating everything from revolution to erotic free love. One finds almost no attractive, well-written paperbacks or pamphlets on "our side." It will be difficult to compete with an Eldridge Cleaver or even a Charles Reich for reader attention, but unless the effort is made -- on a large enough scale and with appropriate imagination to assure some success -- this opportunity for educating the public will be irretrievably lost.

Paid Advertisements

Business pays hundreds of millions of dollars to the media for advertisements. Most of this supports specific products; much of it supports institutional image making; and some fraction of it does support the system. But the latter has been more or less tangential, and rarely part of a sustained, major effort to inform and enlighten the American people.

If American business devoted only 10% of its total annual advertising budget to this overall purpose, it would be a statesman-like expenditure.

The Neglected Political Arena

In the final analysis, the payoff -- short-of revolution -- is what government does. Business has been the favorite whipping-boy of many politicians for many years. But the measure of how far this has gone is perhaps best found in the anti-business views now being expressed by several leading candidates for President of the United States.

It is still Marxist doctrine that the "capitalist" countries are controlled by big business. This doctrine, consistently a part of leftist propaganda all over the world, has a wide public following among Americans.

Yet, as every business executive knows, few elements of American society today have as little influence in government as the American businessman, the corporation, or even the millions of corporate stockholders. If one doubts this, let him undertake the role of "lobbyist" for the business point of view before Congressional committees. The same situation obtains in the legislative halls of most states and major cities. One does not exaggerate to say that, in terms of political influence with respect to the course of legislation and government action, the American business executive is truly the "forgotten man."

Current examples of the impotency of business, and of the near-contempt with which businessmen's views are held, are the stampedes by politicians to support almost any legislation related to "consumerism" or to the "environment."

Politicians reflect what they believe to be majority views of their constituents. It is thus evident that most politicians are making the judgment that the public has little sympathy for the businessman or his viewpoint.

The educational programs suggested above would be designed to enlighten public thinking -- not so much about the businessman and his individual role as about the system which he administers, and which provides the goods, services and jobs on which our country depends.

But one should not postpone more direct political action, while awaiting the gradual change in public opinion to be effected through education and information. Business must learn the lesson, long ago learned by labor and other self-interest groups. This is the lesson that political power is necessary; that such power must be assidously (sic) cultivated; and that when necessary, it must be used aggressively and with determination -- without embarrassment and without the reluctance which has been so characteristic of American business.

As unwelcome as it may be to the Chamber, it should consider assuming a broader and more vigorous role in the political arena.

Neglected Opportunity in the Courts

American business and the enterprise system have been affected as much by the courts as by the executive and legislative branches of government. Under our constitutional system, especially with an activist-minded Supreme Court, the judiciary may be the most important instrument for social, economic and political change.

Other organizations and groups, recognizing this, have been far more astute in exploiting judicial action than American business. Perhaps the most active exploiters of the judicial system have been groups ranging in political orientation from "liberal" to the far left.

The American Civil Liberties Union is one example. It initiates or intervenes in scores of cases each year, and it files briefs amicus curiae in the Supreme Court in a number of cases during each term of that court. Labor unions, civil rights groups and now the public interest law firms are extremely active in the judicial arena. Their success, often at business' expense, has not been inconsequential.

This is a vast area of opportunity for the Chamber, if it is willing to undertake the role of spokesman for American business and if, in turn, business is willing to provide the funds.

As with respect to scholars and speakers, the Chamber would need a highly competent staff of lawyers. In special situations it should be authorized to engage, to appear as counsel amicus in the Supreme Court, lawyers of national standing and reputation. The greatest care should be exercised in selecting the cases in which to participate, or the suits to institute. But the opportunity merits the necessary effort.

Neglected Stockholder Power

The average member of the public thinks of "business" as an impersonal corporate entity, owned by the very rich and managed by over-paid executives. There is an almost total failure to appreciate that "business" actually embraces -- in one way or another -- most Americans. Those for whom business provides jobs, constitute a fairly obvious class. But the 20 million stockholders -- most of whom are of modest means -- are the real owners, the real entrepreneurs, the real capitalists under our system. They provide the capital which fuels the economic system which has produced the highest standard of living in all history. Yet, stockholders have been as ineffectual as business executives in promoting a genuine understanding of our system or in exercising political influence.

The question which merits the most thorough examination is how can the weight and influence of stockholders -- 20 million voters -- be mobilized to support (i) an educational program and (ii) a political action program.

Individual corporations are now required to make numerous reports to shareholders. Many corporations also have expensive "news" magazines which go to employees and stockholders. These opportunities to communicate can be used far more effectively as educational media.

The corporation itself must exercise restraint in undertaking political action and must, of course, comply with applicable laws. But is it not feasible -- through an affiliate of the Chamber or otherwise -- to establish a national organization of American stockholders and give it enough muscle to be influential?

A More Aggressive Attitude

Business interests -- especially big business and their national trade organizations -- have tried to maintain low profiles, especially with respect to political action.

As suggested in the Wall Street Journal article, it has been fairly characteristic of the average business executive to be tolerant -- at least in public -- of those who attack his corporation and the system. Very few businessmen or business organizations respond in kind. There has been a disposition to appease; to regard the opposition as willing to compromise, or as likely to fade away in due time.

Business has shunted confrontation politics. Business, quite understandably, has been repelled by the multiplicity of non-negotiable "demands" made constantly by self-interest groups of all kinds.

While neither responsible business interests, nor the United States Chamber of Commerce, would engage in the irresponsible tactics of some pressure groups, it is essential that spokesmen for the enterprise system -- at all levels and at every opportunity -- be far more aggressive than in the past.

There should be no hesitation to attack the Naders, the Marcuses and others who openly seek destruction of the system. There should not be the slightest hesitation to press vigorously in all political arenas for support of the enterprise system. Nor should there be reluctance to penalize politically those who oppose it.

Lessons can be learned from organized labor in this respect. The head of the AFL-CIO may not appeal to businessmen as the most endearing or public-minded of citizens. Yet, over many years the heads of national labor organizations have done what they were paid to do very effectively. They may not have been beloved, but they have been respected -- where it counts the most -- by politicians, on the campus, and among the media.

It is time for American business -- which has demonstrated the greatest capacity in all history to produce and to influence consumer decisions -- to apply their great talents vigorously to the preservation of the system itself.

The Cost

The type of program described above (which includes a broadly based combination of education and political action), if undertaken long term and adequately staffed, would require far more generous financial support from American corporations than the Chamber has ever received in the past. High level management participation in Chamber affairs also would be required.

The staff of the Chamber would have to be significantly increased, with the highest quality established and maintained. Salaries would have to be at levels fully comparable to those paid key business executives and the most prestigious faculty members. Professionals of the great skill in advertising and in working with the media, speakers, lawyers and other specialists would have to be recruited.

It is possible that the organization of the Chamber itself would benefit from restructuring. For example, as suggested by union experience, the office of President of the Chamber might well be a full-time career position. To assure maximum effectiveness and continuity, the chief executive officer of the Chamber should not be changed each year. The functions now largely performed by the President could be transferred to a Chairman of the Board, annually elected by the membership. The Board, of course, would continue to exercise policy control.

Quality Control is Essential

Essential ingredients of the entire program must be responsibility and "quality control." The publications, the articles, the speeches, the media programs, the advertising, the briefs filed in courts, and the appearances before legislative committees -- all must meet the most exacting standards of accuracy and professional excellence. They must merit respect for their level of public responsibility and scholarship, whether one agrees with the viewpoints expressed or not.

Relationship to Freedom

The threat to the enterprise system is not merely a matter of economics. It also is a threat to individual freedom.

It is this great truth -- now so submerged by the rhetoric of the New Left and of many liberals -- that must be re-affirmed if this program is to be meaningful.

There seems to be little awareness that the only alternatives to free enterprise are varying degrees of bureaucratic regulation of individual freedom -- ranging from that under moderate socialism to the iron heel of the leftist or rightist dictatorship.

We in America already have moved very far indeed toward

some aspects of state socialism, as the needs and complexities of a vast urban society require types of regulation and control that were quite unnecessary in earlier times. In some areas, such regulation and control already have seriously impaired the freedom of both business and labor, and indeed of the public generally. But most of the essential freedoms remain: private ownership, private profit, labor unions, collective bargaining, consumer choice, and a market economy in which competition largely determines price, quality and variety of the goods and services provided the consumer.

In addition to the ideological attack on the system itself (discussed in this memorandum), its essentials also are threatened by inequitable taxation, and -- more recently -- by an inflation which has seemed uncontrollable.14 But whatever the causes of diminishing economic freedom may be, the truth is that freedom as a concept is indivisible. As the experience of the socialist and totalitarian states demonstrates, the contraction and denial of economic freedom is followed inevitably by governmental restrictions on other cherished rights. It is this message, above all others, that must be carried home to the American people.

Conclusion

It hardly need be said that the views expressed above are tentative and suggestive. The first step should be a thorough study. But this would be an exercise in futility unless the Board of Directors of the Chamber accepts the fundamental premise of this paper, namely, that business and the enterprise system are in deep trouble, and the hour is late.

Footnotes

1. Variously called: the "free enterprise system," "capitalism," and the "profit system." The American political system of democracy under the rule of law is also under attack, often by the same individuals and organizations who seek to undermine the enterprise system.

2. Richmond News Leader, June 8, 1970. Column of William F. Buckley, Jr.

3. N.Y. Times Service article, reprinted Richmond Times-Dispatch, May 17, 1971.

4. Stewart Alsop, Yale and the Deadly Danger, Newsweek, May 18. 1970.

5. Editorial, Richmond Times-Dispatch, July 7, 1971.

6. Dr. Milton Friedman, Prof. of Economics, U. of Chicago, writing a foreword to Dr. Arthur A. Shenfield's Rockford College lectures entitled "The Ideological War Against Western Society," copyrighted 1970 by Rockford College.

7. Fortune. May, 1971, p. 145. This Fortune analysis of the Nader influence includes a reference to Nader's visit to a college where he was paid a lecture fee of $2,500 for "denouncing America's big corporations in venomous language . . . bringing (rousing and spontaneous) bursts of applause" when he was asked when he planned to run for President.

8. The Washington Post, Column of William Raspberry, June 28, 1971.

9. Jeffrey St. John, The Wall Street Journal, May 21, 1971.

* . Italic emphasis added by Mr. Powell.

10. Barron's National Business and Financial Weekly, "The Total Break with America, The Fifth Annual Conference of Socialist Scholars," Sept. 15, 1969.

11. On many campuses freedom of speech has been denied to all who express moderate or conservative viewpoints.

12. It has been estimated that the evening half-hour news programs of the networks reach daily some 50,000,000 Americans.

13. One illustration of the type of article which should not go unanswered appeared in the popular "The New York" of July 19,

1971. This was entitled "A Populist Manifesto" by ultra liberal Jack Newfield -- who argued that "the root need in our country is 'to redistribute wealth'."

14. The recent "freeze" of prices and wages may well be justified by the current inflationary crisis. But if imposed as a permanent measure the enterprise system will have sustained a near fatal blow.

IN CONCLUSION

Just as Thomas Paine laid the blame directly on King George, I lay the blame for our current mess directly upon the new kings, specifically, the inheritance generation who were given everything and expect even more. For just as the privileged royalty before them did, they have greedily taken all for themselves at the expense of the common family. Wealth concentration and income disparity are at record levels (IRS).

It is difficult to retain faith in those who knowingly and willingly engage in deception for their sole financial benefit. I was not raised that way. Apparently some of America's most wealthy citizens were. No one wants to deny honest gains to those who earn them, but for decades now, an undue share of benefits has gone to the holders of capital, and policy decisions have created and sustained that inequity. The supply-side lie is alive and well because of the efforts of some of the wealthiest Americans. They have embraced and promoted this lie with full knowledge of its dubious claims.

The Powell memo doesn't counsel lying, but it strongly suggests aggressive advocacy of their positions, which would not be a problem were the positions based upon factual evidence. But they were not and are not so based. Over the years, evidence has emerged that many policy decisions were promoted with known mis- and disinformation originating from the think tanks spawned during the mid-1970's. These Powell-inspired think tanks continue to script false narratives to protect ill-gotten benefits. Corporate-owned media messages are carefully planned and strictly followed. It is not by chance that the same phrases, the same talking points are heard simultaneously from varied sources. The framing of policy disagreements with half-truths, wrongly portraying honest Americans as something less than honest, is beyond the pale. Evidently, that's the only way to sell the supply-side lie. Such is the world in which we live. Journalism wasn't always this way. Truth used to trump volume. It no longer does.

It doesn't have to remain like this. As citizens, we can change things. That's the beauty of the Constitution. We may never get dishonest ideologues to tell the truth, but we may able to stop them from buying the instruments to disseminate their lies. We must get money out of politics. Our future depends upon it. We must expose the deceit, by boycotting those businesses (program advertisers) that promote it. We must end the supply-side lie.

And the following is how to achieve it:

1) End corporate personhood. Then, get money out of politics. Support the 28th amendment movement.

2) Insist on factual correctness from public airwaves media sources through the license renewal process. FOX, Clear Channel, and other ideological bound broadcasters are required to operate in the public interest, not to operate in pure ideological interest; hold them to their requirement or revoke their licenses.

3) Reinvest in infrastructure – specifically a new, efficient electric grid. Put America to work rebuilding our crumbling infrastructure and fund it with a financial transaction tax on Wall Street speculators.

4) Progressive tax reform--return to '93 Deficit Reduction rates for upper incomes & add a financial transaction tax (make Wall Street pay for malfeasance). Tax investments equally, it's income.

5) Reinstate Glass-Steagal and break-up "too big to fail" entities (Voelker Rule).

6) Renegotiate unfair trade deals, insisting on fair trade for labor and the environment.

7) VOTE – and get others to vote against the purveyors of deceit.

8) OCCUPIERS!   Follow these (hiking etiquette) rules when occupying:

   - leave no sign and do no harm

   - pack it in, pack it out

ABOUT THE AUTHOR

I was born in Grand Rapids, Minnesota in 1954, the second of six boys to Lewis and Caroline Straka. My first recollections were from St. Peter, Minnesota, the community in which I was raised through high school ('72 grad). I jumped between college and work during most of the mid-1970's, celebrating the end of the Vietnam War and trying to settle on a career path. The relief of not being drafted in '72-'73 and the imminent end of the draft was reason to recalibrate.

I lived with old friends and new friends. Roomies Jim and Tom worked as child counselors at St. Joe's Children's Home in Minneapolis. I volunteered and strongly considered a career in social work. We played co-ed volleyball for St. Joe's and tipped a few after each event. One of our teammates was Louie Anderson, before he became a famous comedian. His court skills were of no concern. He was funny, and has proved it since. I remember his amateur nights at Mickey Finn's. Who knew? None of my roomies or Louie of course, are child counselors anymore. They couldn't raise families on those wages. Too bad, they were good.

By the late 1970's, I'd determined that broadcast journalism was the path to pursue. I attended Brown Institute in Minneapolis, (graduating in 1981), and quickly began my journalism career as an airborne (plane or helicopter) news reporter for Metro Traffic Control.

In 1982, I moved to Montana. I worked in radio for four years, before returning to Minnesota to add undergraduate degrees in Business Administration and Marketing/Public Relations from Minnesota State University in 1987. During school, I instructed classes at the local access television studio, teaching electronic news gathering and production to college students.

After a couple of years as Direct Marketing manager for a growing high tech firm in Minneapolis, I again returned (1989) to my beloved mountains in Montana. Following a year lobbying with NFIB, I resumed my media (TV) career for a few years until I saw the writing on the wall. Media consolidation was decimating both quality and opportunity. So I enrolled in school at the University of

Montana ('94-'95) in their MBA program. Since, I've been self-employed and a small business owner, but I have not lost my love for honest journalism. I write and research for fun, just as I hike, climb, and photograph for fun. Glacier Park is my church. It is where I attend services. Its "steeples" and whispering streams beckon me always. It is where I find peace and clarity.

Author atop Scenic Point (seated) and Mt. Pollock (standing) in Glacier Park
– photos by author

IN MEMORIAM - FOR MOM

Everything I am, I owe to my Mom (and Dad), and she knew that before she recently passed away, just days after this past Christmas (2011). Thankfully we did get to spend one more Christmas as a family, but not without Mom's objection to the night nurse that, "I wish my family didn't have to see me in this hellhole". That's my Mom. She was always thinking of others first, teaching a lesson in dignity, even as she lay dying. What she probably didn't realize is that there was no other place I'd rather be, than by her side offering love and comfort as she passed to her new world. I'll miss her, but will always have her with me.

Over the years and the miles, we grew separately yet together, respecting each other's individuality. We encouraged each other's endeavors. We recognized each other's shared values and talked often as to how to attain them. We were close friends who could talk about anything and everything. We river rafted, cross country skied, and hiked Glacier Park together during her visits. We even survived an F3 tornado huddled together in the back room of a restaurant with no basement. We enjoyed each other's company immensely. Even though our opinions slightly differed, our intended shared outcome of creating a better future for her children and her children's children was never in question. We agreed that other people matter.

In our last conversation, before her sudden illness, her last words to me were, "Write that book, Jerry". I'd told her my plans to publish my observations. She knew my purpose was to make the world better for her children and her children's children. Again, she was thinking of others. That's my Mom. I can only hope to be half the loving person she was. I miss you, Caroline Straka. Every day.

www.ingramcontent.com/pod-product-compliance
Lightning Source LLC
Chambersburg PA
CBHW050411290526
45786CB00003B/1214